LANDSCAPE MODELLING

by Barry Norman

Wild Swan Publications Ltd.

ISBN 0 906867 44 4

For

GILL

ACKNOWLEDGEMENTS

The seeds were sown for this book in the days when I was packed off to the Model Railway Club's Easter Exhibition by my Mum and Dad. I would like to thank them for the support they have given me over the years and particularly to my Mum for typing this manuscript. The work of correcting, reading and guiding the draft of this book has fallen to my wife Gill who is often taken for granted in the preparation of Petherick for exhibitions. Without her support I doubt whether this model could have been built, and I would like to record my appreciation of the many times when it is too easy for me to forget that I didn't do it all on my own.

Thanks must also go to Bob Cockcroft for taking several of the photographs under the most difficult of conditions and to Bob Barlow for writing a foreword that reflects so concisely the mood of this book and my feelings. Lastly, I must thank Paul Karau and June Judge as I feel very proud that my photographs, drawings and text should be treated with such sensitivity, perception and untiring care, to produce a book that turns my dreams into reality.　BARRY NORMAN

Photos by the author unless otherwise shown.

Designed by Paul Karau
Typeset by Berkshire Publishing Services
Printed by The Amadeus Press Ltd, Huddersfield

Published by
WILD SWAN PUBLICATIONS LTD.
1-3 Hagbourne Road, Didcot, Oxon OX11 8DP

Foreword

At exhibitions up and down the country, many thousands of people have seen Barry Norman's masterpiece model railway, 'Petherick'. Some, like me, have gladly travelled many miles for the privilege, such is the magnetism of the miniature slice of bygone Cornwall that is 'Petherick'. Indeed, the layout's enormous public success is Barry's main qualification for writing this book and if, after reading it, you find yourself able to apply a few new techniques and artistic flourishes to your own model railway, its purpose will have been served well enough.

However, there's far more to this slim volume than useful modeller's hints and wrinkles; there is a deeper dimension which speaks of success out of failure, of observation blending with a determination to get things *right*, and, above all, of love for the subject — in this case, our own British landscape. Looking around and loving what you see is a taller order than taking it for granted as most of us do, especially when those surroundings are conventionally 'ugly' like so many urban landscapes today. But somewhere, even in the grimmest of city wastes, beauty exists. And if you're out there studying the landscape closely enough — in order to build an accurate model, for example — you will assuredly find it. Not just once, but dozens of times: images that will linger and give inner pleasure for many, many years. I find it comforting that this hobby of ours — which most will concede is a fairly insignificant part of whatever great scheme exists — can lead us to greater insights into our relationship with our own small planet.

Heady stuff, indeed, but not so ethereal when couched in terms of questions: How green is grass? How do animals exist in the fields? How is one tree different from another? These are not extracts from a psychologist's encounter group session, but from a modeller's notebook — questions that must be answered if our models are to succeed. Our motives may be different from the psychologist's — we need to colour our lint grass, deploy our plastic cows correctly and differentiate an ash from a beech — but the answers themselves are no less profound. And we end up enriching ourselves as well as our models.

Of course, converting images to three-dimensional miniatures is easier said than done. Books, especially when they are as well-crafted as this one, are a great help, because they can eliminate some of the mistakes inherent in trail-blazing. For 'Petherick' is a success because Barry Norman failed; in the first instance (and often in the second, third and fourth) he failed to get his grass the right colour, his trees the correct shape, his cornfields the right height, his stonework the proper texture, and so on. Fortunately for us, he trudged on, continuing to interpret the images and trying new techniques and materials until the results satisfied him.

All this — this blend of loving observation and doggedly-practised artistry — was poured into 'Petherick', a sleepy LSWR station nestling in a shallow valley feeding the River Camel somewhere between Wadebridge and Padstow. And now, too, it has been poured into this book.

In expressing his habitually polite wish that spectators enjoy his layout, Barry always says: 'You may not hear the seagulls calling as they fly in from their fishing grounds, or smell fresh mackerel on the salty air . . .' to which I will add: Look long enough, and you just might!

Bob Barlow
Editor of Model Railway Journal

A chilly summer's morn in Cornwall.

Introduction

A thrush sits in the comfort of an ash tree, singing his morning song as the branches sway to the rhythm of the breeze, and sunlight plays through dancing clouds onto a nearby station platform. Corn rustles, the stream glitters and gurgles, and cattle leave tracks in the dew on a meadow of golden buttercups. A chilly summer's morn in Cornwall.

This is a rather lyrical way to set the scene, but it suits my purpose, for I believe there's more to modelling a railway than just the railway itself. I try to see it in a far fuller and deeper sense — the complete picture of a railway as a part of its surrounding landscape.

And there are many different landscapes: swathes of heather-clad moorland, where crows wheel overhead; dark, rich marshes and fens, where skylarks hover in the endless sky; limestone peaks and crags, where falcons rule; orchards and meadowlands, home to hordes of squabbling sparrows.

Railways have distinctive locations, the nature and character of which are as crucial as the identity of the lines themselves. Indeed, the landscape — and yes, even the birdlife — contribute to that identity in a massive and fundamental way, inseparable from the railway weaving through it. Just as the Highland Railway's metals traversed braes and burns, pine woods and glowering distilleries, so the South Eastern Railway's identity is inextricably linked to red brick oast houses, hop fields and orchards.

Seeing all this and bringing it to life under one's own hands can do so much to enrich our models; it can say far more about the location of a station than the railway can by itself. It may be easy to identify a London and North Western station by its shiplapped buildings, its signals and signal boxes — but surround it with dry stone walls, a shelter belt of trees, a lone limestone haybarn, and it must be in Derbyshire.

Studying the landscape surrounding the railway, and trying to capture that natural character in miniature, is challenging and rewarding and will result in a more complete, authentic and interesting model. That, I hope, will be the message of this book.

BARRY NORMAN

S. H. FREESE

A pre-war glimpse of rural Suffolk at Thorington ford and footbridge.

CHAPTER ONE

Planning a Model Landscape

AN APPROACH TO THE DESIGN

A convincing model must reflect the chosen prototype although this need not be interpreted as the exact copy of any one station. However, it is a good idea to have one in mind. Usually what is modelled is a compromise between the information that has been gathered, a guess at what it may have been like in the period that one wishes to model, and the constraints of size imposed by its home in the 'railway room'. To make an exact copy of a station can be an impracticable task. Its atmosphere is more important than slavish accuracy.

Just as a station may need altering in size or complexity within the bounds of railway practice, so too will the landscape. To represent the mountain country of the Highlands of Scotland, pine clad hillsides, heather and gorse will help to convey the right atmosphere. It is therefore important to look for and analyse those features that seem typical or even unique to the area being modelled. It is only with an empathy for the whole scene, and the ability to discriminate and identify the most characterful details, that the appropriate atmosphere is recreated.

Buildings, of course, help to add character to the setting. A distillery, an oast house or a windmill are obvious indications of where the layout may be. Brick, limestone, granite or timber capture the traditional building materials of a county. Timber-framed farmhouses washed in Suffolk pink, contrast with the timber-clad cottages of Kent, or the darkening sandstones of Yorkshire.

The use of the land varies. The fertile arable land of East Anglia contrasts with the livestock farming of the West Country. The balance between crops and pasture should also be considered and in this context the period being modelled is another factor.

Land use has changed much in this century with the loss of pasture and meadow land to arable crops. The techniques of farming have developed rapidly from the horse-drawn plough, through the age of the steam engine, to the tractors

and harvesters of today. The time in history or period of the model depends on more than just the dress of the people, and the vehicles on the roads.

As the seasons pass the whole appearance of the countryside changes. Trees lose their leaves, and colours become mute and dull in winter; with the vivid brightness of spring, hedgerows come into leaf, followed by the May blossom and cow parsley, delicate in its cobweb of whiteness. These and many more features can add a seasonal dialogue to a model. Fields once under plough, scattered with rusty coloured leaves turning yellow in the early morning mists, disappear as bright green shoots colour the land. These

are all important factors in establishing an authentic and atmospheric model.

Consideration for the geographical, architectural, historical and seasonal aspects of our heritage can offer a far more challenging, rewarding and worthwhile approach to model making.

DESIGNING THE LANDSCAPE

It may seem strange to suggest designing a landscape, but a far more convincing picture will result if some thought is put into its composition. Perhaps if I could find that 'right' station surrounded by a landscape that was both interesting and filled with an empathy for its environment, I would certainly model it. Inevit-

A place, a season, a time, important elements in establishing an authentic model.
S. H. FREESE

1

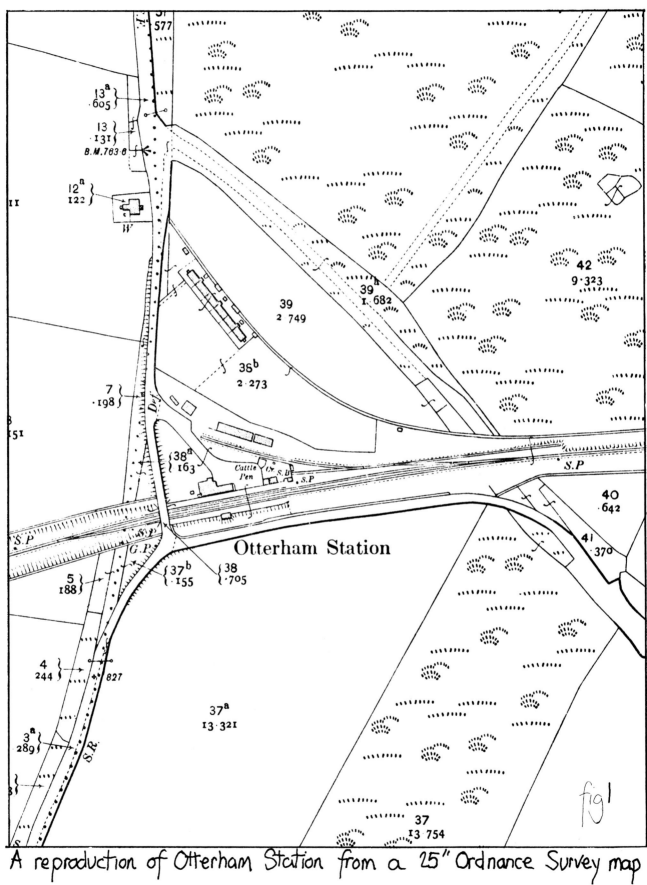

A reproduction of Otterham Station from a 25″ Ordnance Survey map

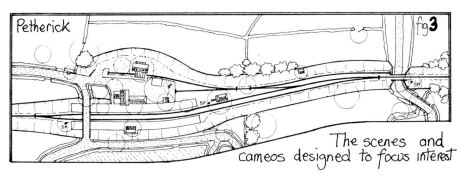

Petherick fig 3

The scenes and cameos designed to focus interest

ably this is just not so. Stations need to be compressed, often they look better like that in model form, and this enables them to fit into the 'railway room'. By cutting and changing the real thing there need not be any loss of realism. What is needed is atmosphere, a feeling for the station, the railway company and its train services.

If your model is to be based on a prototype then a track plan and photographs are essential before a start can be made. This information can often be found in one of the excellent and growing range of more recent railway books from specialist publishers. Even some of the more general track plan books can provide much inspiration but if you are lucky you may even discover that your chosen prototype has appeared in one of the more detailed studies which often include a wealth of information, photographs and drawings. However, the track plan for Petherick, which was that of Otterham station (*Fig. 1*) came from the British Museum Map Library. A written request will open the doors to a host of 25 inch Ordnance Survey maps. These can be viewed in large books, and provide quite a comprehensive insight into the cartographic surveys of our countryside. Different editions update the changes that occur; I used a 2nd Edition dated 1907.

Looking at the plan it is often possible to shorten sidings and loops (*Fig. 2*), to introduce any desired compression without any loss of character. Interesting railway features become more related, and space need not obviously be removed.

Once the track plan is finalised the landscape comes under consideration. I have mentioned the need to think about those typical or unique features that characterise an area. Whether it be dry stone walls with limestone haybarns, or cob and thatch cottages amidst rolling

pastures. However, placing these features interestingly yet realistically needs some thought. I always think of a model as a series of scenes or cameos (*Fig. 3*). Each forms a focal point which attracts the eye, and a platform from which to leap to the next scene. The eye will then travel meaningfully from one end of the layout

to the other without wandering lost over a scene offering little visual direction.

This approach is dramatised when the model is deliberately designed to channel your vision (*Fig. 4*). A lane can be angled so that a view along it takes the eye towards an interesting scene. Trees can be placed so that they tunnel your vision between them; it is also wise to force viewing angles by not making everything obvious from one viewpoint. Trees, buildings or hills somehow ask the viewer to peer around them, breaking up the general field of vision. A tree may seem in the way at the front of the model, but it achieves purpose by forcing the viewer to change his viewing position. All this is very much more apparent on a broad landscape when it is a delight to see the way in which different objects appear to move in relation to one another.

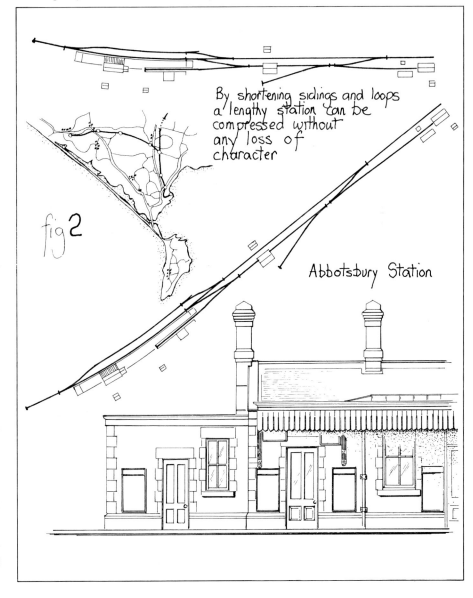

By shortening sidings and loops a lengthy station can be compressed without any loss of character

fig 2

Abbotsbury Station

Although a train might be the focal point of the whole model, I am always keen to hide it partly from view. It is far more interesting to see it peeping above cuttings, bursting under a bridge, hiding behind trees, and then towering above meadows on an embankment. Variety and interest are the keys to success, and the right combination can turn a seemingly dull model into a challenging assault course for your eyes.

So this is my approach to landscape modelling — simply an empathy with the railway and its landscape in time and season, with the model designed to draw the eye, challenging it to perceive the interesting, and educating it to see more widely.

FINALISING THE DESIGN

As this philosophy stimulates ideas, these need to be interpreted into practical model making. A little more information is probably required, like photographs of the station, and its surroundings.

A field trip to the site will reveal much about its environment. Decisions can then be reached about any alterations that need to be made. Exploration of the surrounding landscape will inspire ideas for scenic model making as interesting

features will be revealed, and a host of information assembled, from which the model can be designed.

It is a good idea to build in miniature a version of the final model, to test out ideas (*Fig. 4a*). It is not easy thinking about a 3-D landscape and trying to convey your thoughts on paper. I find it easier to think by working with something more tangible in front of me.

Start by drawing the trackplan to a smaller scale on some thick card. This can then be cut out and surrounded by the landscape, using polystyrene ceiling tiles, shaped until the topography of the area is captured. This is a quick way of looking at the third dimension, plenty of failures will be made upon the way, but it is better to iron out problems in this scale, rather than on the completed model.

Onto this basic land shape it is helpful to add small blocks of balsa to represent buildings and lumps of lichen for hedges and trees. Look at eye level from one end of the model to the other. Think, does it look right? Does it look real? Does it look convincing? If the answers are yes, we can move to the actual construction. A vision becomes reality, and vague ideas are transferred to hard facts, as we move on to baseboard construction.

Although a train might be the focal point of the whole model, it is far more interesting to see it peeping above cuttings, bursting under bridges, or hiding behind trees. A well planned layout will enrich the visual impact of the trains that run upon it.

Designing the layout to make it visually interesting

fig 4

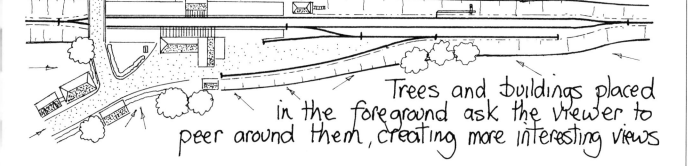

Trees and buildings placed in the foreground ask the viewer to peer around them, creating more interesting views

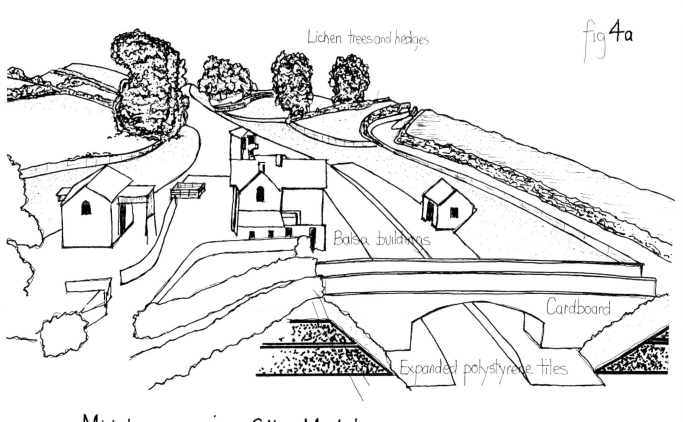

fig 4a

Lichen trees and hedges

Balsa buildings

Cardboard

Expanded polystyrene tiles

Miniature version of the Model

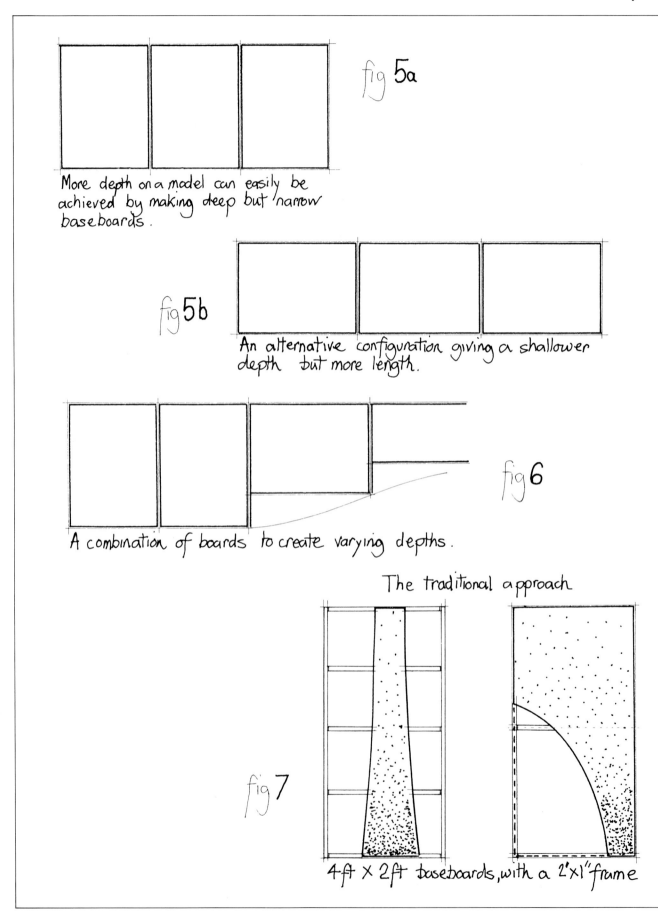

fig 5a

More depth on a model can easily be achieved by making deep but narrow baseboards.

fig 5b

An alternative configuration giving a shallower depth but more length.

fig 6

A combination of boards to create varying depths.

The traditional approach

fig 7

4ft × 2ft baseboards, with a 2″×1″ frame

CHAPTER TWO

Baseboards

STRENGTH, WEIGHT AND SIZE

In the last century navvies were carving our railways through the landscape, filling trucks with spoil. A hill would have been sliced by a cutting, and a valley filled by an embankment, but engineers tried to survey and design their railways so that they took the flattest route through the countryside. Thus railways often twisted and turned to avoid hills and the need to tunnel and build viaducts.

Our start is with a flat base and the modeller's task is to create a landscape that looks as though it was already in existence before the railway. We may need to build a cutting or embankment, or perhaps a viaduct towering over a stream nestling in the valley below. We must therefore look for a way of building baseboards that are adaptable, and enable us to build easily just what we want. Our choice also needs to consider strength, weight and size. The strength of a baseboard is the most important. The problems caused if it should twist or warp once it is built can prove disastrous and cause the builder to lose heart and deflate his enthusiasm. Track can only be laid on a flat base, but more importantly, it must remain flat month after month, year after year. Allowance must also be made for some tough treatment, the unexpected knock or accident.

Strength and weight are often linked, the ideal is to increase the former by decreasing the latter. However, the greatest proportion of the weight is always in the top surface (particularly if chipboard is used), which leads one to consider the virtues of an open top form of construction.

As for size, it is difficult to come to any single answer. The boards must relate to the design of the layout, and it may not always be convenient to divide the plan into a set number of equal sections. Joints between boards have to avoid turnouts and their motors and ideally they have to be in an appropriate position so that they can be disguised in some way by the scenery. However, I do think that if there is a variation in the size of each board, it is wise to arrange them in pairs. Thus if your model is to be stored or

exhibited it can be stacked by bolting a pair of boards face to face. This will protect all the fine detail that will follow. A permanent layout is also better built in manageable sections, as this will make construction much easier. Each board can then be removed and placed in a convenient position to work upon.

It was once said that 2 ft by 4 ft was the ideal size. This I would argue is far too small when adding depth and trying to make the railway rightfully appear part of its surroundings. So what is the ideal? A 5 ft length will fit the width of a small van or length of a hatchback, and a 3 ft width will drop between the wheel arches of a car. Thus for a portable layout, 5 ft by 3 ft would seem reasonable. However, 4 ft by 3 ft may be preferred (*Figs. 5a & 5b*) if it is to be carried down stairs and through cottage doors, especially if bolted to another board. For a permanent layout it is probably near the ideal, but an extra 6 inches in width may give just that bit more depth. However, a combination of boards could be arranged to produce a more useful depth of between 3 and 6 feet (*Fig. 6*).

THE METHOD OF CONSTRUCTION

The most commonly used method of building baseboards is to cut lengths of 2 in. x 1 in. pine, gluing and screwing them into a simple framework (*Fig. 7*). That's fine if you can find straight pieces of pine and then guarantee that they will not warp or twist. I thought and thought about developing a system that could be adapted to all the possible needs of the

model railway, yet retain the simplicity of the 2 in. x 1 in. framework. To overcome the inherent desire to twist and move, I looked at plywood. This is often built into what has been known as an eggbox construction, a rather strange shaped eggbox that gains its strength from a triangulated framework (*Fig. 8*). This gives a rigidity to the thin flexible plywood strips cut for the sides. I wasn't too happy with this method, although it is quite successful on small boards. It is a complex idea, particularly on larger boards, and not a system that lends itself easily to open scenic work and a wide range of constructions, like embankments, valleys and hillsides. No doubt these problems could be overcome, but I felt something simpler could be designed, so I thought why not copy the pine framework, but replace the pine with a simple plywood construction, and the ideal may be found.

The question of experimenting with ideas and then putting them into practice on a layout is important. Unless an idea is proved by the rigours of layout building over a period of time, it cannot be considered a success. After many exhibitions with Petherick, this method of building baseboards has proved very reliable.

Thus each piece of 2 in. x 1 in. is replaced by a side member which is made by sandwiching blocks of pine between two strips of ply (*Fig. 9*). This is really based upon the canterlever bridge principle, if one strip is in tension then the other must be in compression. In practice two flimsy strips of ply become rigid and

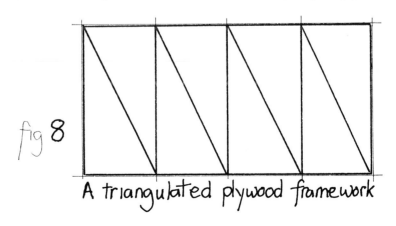

fig 8

A triangulated plywood framework

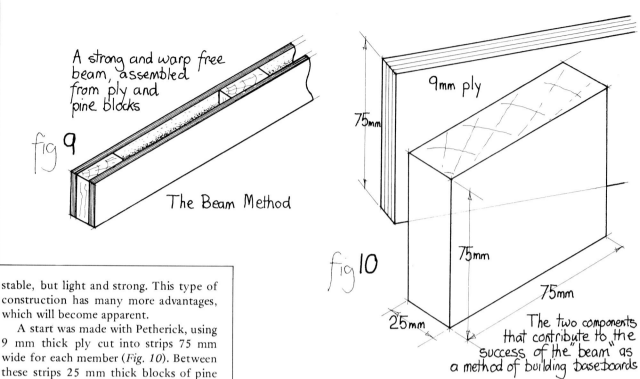

A strong and warp free beam, assembled from ply and pine blocks

fig 9

The Beam Method

9mm ply

75mm

75mm

75mm

25mm

fig 10

The two components that contribute to the success of the "beam" as a method of building baseboards

stable, but light and strong. This type of construction has many more advantages, which will become apparent.

A start was made with Petherick, using 9 mm thick ply cut into strips 75 mm wide for each member (*Fig. 10*). Between these strips 25 mm thick blocks of pine 75 mm square were glued and nailed. I have subsequently tried using 6 mm ply and 12 mm thick blocks, and this appears to be just as successful, but only time, wear and tear will tell.

Start by buying 1 in. thick pine and select a width near to 75 mm. This size is not critical, but it does produce a dimension to which the ply should be cut. Then ask your timber merchant to saw an 8 ft x 4 ft sheet of 9 mm ply into strips to coincide with the pine. The pine is cut into 75 mm squares and the ply to the length of the baseboard before each block is glued and nailed between the strips. I find it easier to knock all the nails into the ply strip before gluing the blocks, and hammering in the nails. It really doesn't matter if the assembled member comes out a little twisted, because once it is dry, it won't move again.

The positioning of the blocks relates to the design of the frame, but try to place them about every 12″-18″. One big advantage of this new approach is that the blocks can be turned to alter the direction of their grain. It is well known that a good screwed joint can only be achieved if the screw is driven into the side grain. It will never grip as satisfactorily in end grain. Thus by placing the grain in the blocks in different directions we can achieve a versatile framework (*Figs. 11 & 12*).

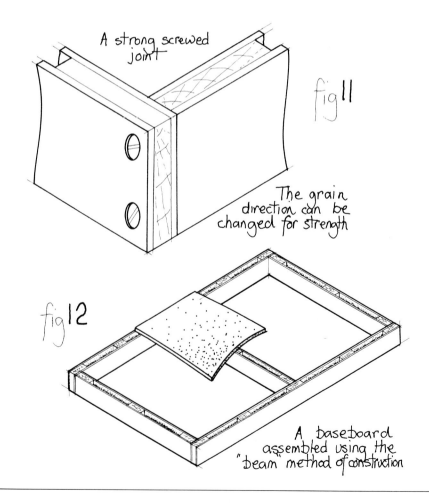

A strong screwed joint

fig 11

The grain direction can be changed for strength

fig 12

A baseboard assembled using the "beam" method of construction

BUILDING THE FRAMEWORK

The simplest way of using these new ply members is the method used on Petherick, and is most suited to a deep and narrow board (*Fig. 13*). However, the cross member that supports the track base can get in the way of point motors and wiring, so it may be better for this to be supported on two cross members (*Fig. 14*). Remember that the chipboard top can be cut over the size of the track bed everywhere except on an embankment. An alternative method is to reverse the direction of the framework, thus making long but narrower boards (*Figs. 15a & 15b*).

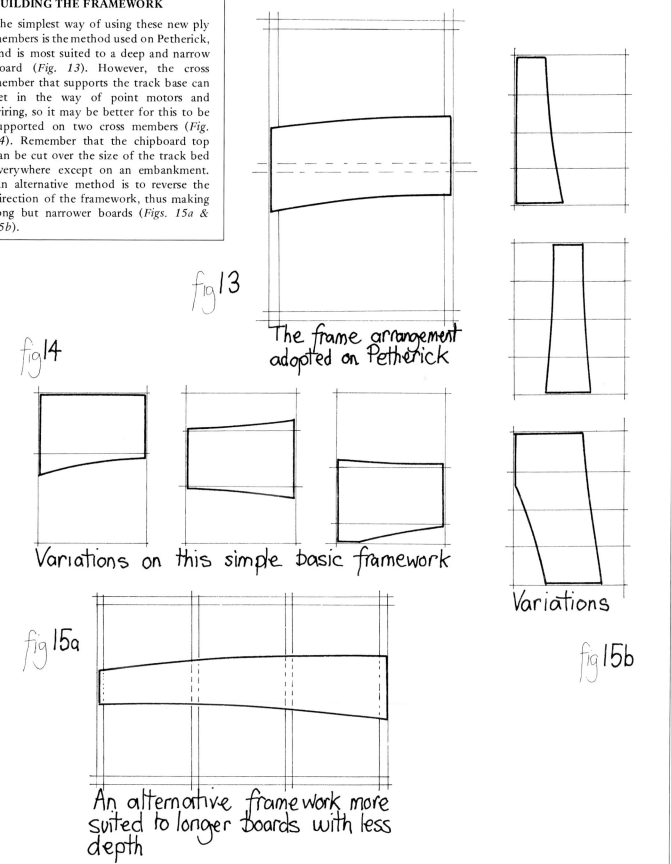

fig 13

The frame arrangement adopted on Petherick

fig 14

Variations on this simple basic framework

Variations

fig 15a

fig 15b

An alternative framework more suited to longer boards with less depth

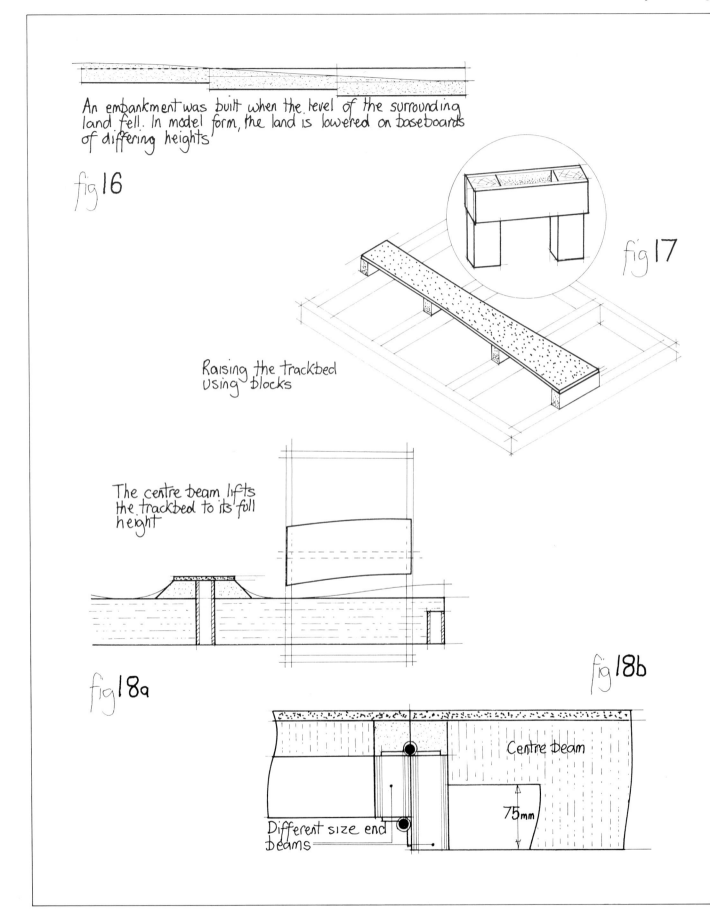

An embankment was built when the level of the surrounding land fell. In model form, the land is lowered on baseboards of differing heights

fig 16

fig 17

Raising the trackbed using blocks

The centre beam lifts the trackbed to its full height

fig 18a

fig 18b

Different size end beams

Centre Beam

75mm

Embankments can be built once the height of the track above the ground level of the hillside on each board is determined (*Fig. 16*). On a gently sloping hillside a modest fall or drop in baseboards of about 1½ in. in every 30 in. would give an embankment similar to the one at Petherick. The track base can be screwed to blocks that slide into the framework (*Fig. 17*). Again here ply strips, carefully cut to a width that matches the fall in the land, sandwich these blocks. However, on the original arrangement of framework (as in Petherick) the embankment is achieved by a slightly different method (*Figs. 18a & 18b*). The width of the cross member is increased to the fall in the land, and the ends matched to the profile of the embankment.

It must be appreciated that building a layout involves much thought in the planning stage. From the track plan and miniature of the model, the height and depth of the land from the track bed is easy to estimate. The baseboards can then be designed to meet the requirements, which generally speaking need not be as diverse as Petherick. Most stations were built in fairly flat locations, a field that could easily be levelled was a good spot. The more interesting and dramatic sections of scenery were more often found along the line. Perhaps that's a pity from our point of view, but it does mean that baseboards are less likely to be too complicated.

All these frames are joined together with 2½ in. No. 8 CSK wood screws, tightened up to compress the PVA glue (Evostik Resin W or Unibond). Make sure that you drill tapping and clearance size holes for each screw, doing the job correctly, as screws are driven easier into the wood with a screwdriver than a hammer! The boards are finished by gluing and nailing (1½ in. ovals) the chipboard surface to the frame.

JOINING BOARDS

There are many ways in which one board can be joined to its neighbour. A pair of bolts and wing nuts can be used, but these offer a poor and inaccurate way of aligning the track. What is needed is a way of clamping tightly, and aligning perfectly, each board every time it is put into position. To my mind, I have never found anything better than split hinges.

For lateral alignment a flap hinge can simply be screwed to each side of the board (*Fig. 19*), but, whilst this aligns the boards well, it still allows them to revolve around the pin, so that the layout will assume the level of the floor. Therefore a better way is to use two sets of hinges on each joint, one at the top, and the other at the bottom (*Fig. 20*). The resulting rigidity prevents any movement and holds the boards horizontal. However, it is only once the boards are clamped together that the hinges can be fitted and tightly screwed into place. Each pin will then be knocked out of position, once the rivet on one end is filed off. The resultant set of boards defy the bumps and hollows in a floor although, of course, the legs may need packing as they will lift off an uneven surface. Thin strips of card or wood can be slipped in the gaps under each leg, which, in my opinion, is much easier than building in spirit levels or adjustable legs.

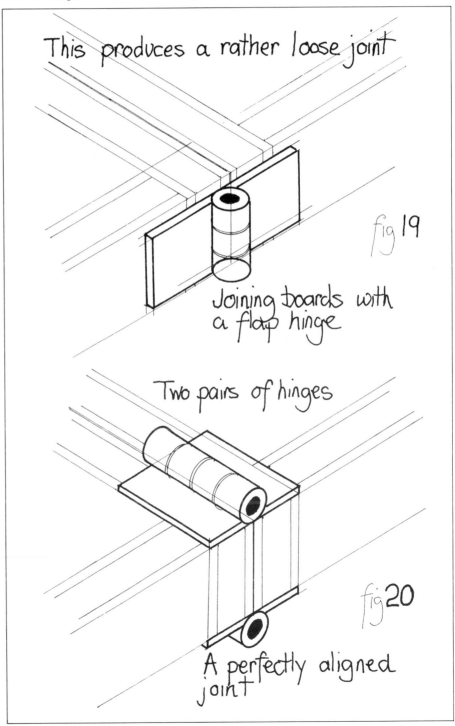

This produces a rather loose joint

fig 19

Joining boards with a flap hinge

Two pairs of hinges

fig 20

A perfectly aligned joint

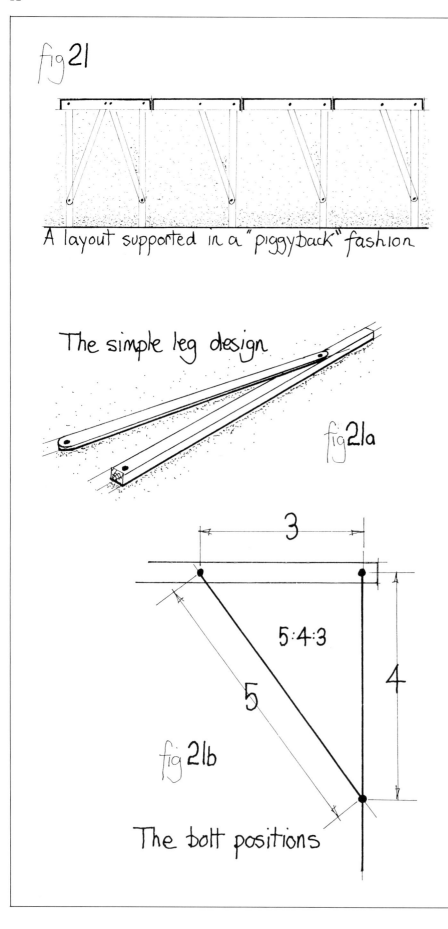

fig 21

A layout supported in a "piggyback" fashion

The simple leg design

fig 21a

3

5:4:3

5

4

fig 21b

The bolt positions

LEGS

Somewhere between your knees and chin is the desired height for the layout. Eye level gives the most realistic viewpoint and I suppose that's what we are trying to recreate, but a model towering 5 ft above the floor doesn't always give that heart-warming impression that we hoped for. I like to be able to gaze at eye level, and also to be able to look slightly down on it. Thus I set the height of Petherick at 3 ft. 9 in., however another 3 in. would please those that are a little taller than my 5 ft 4½ in. Don't expect to find a height at which you can view it, and work on it, it is better to remove sections to a bench or table.

If you have ever taken a layout to an exhibition you will soon find that legs are the most awkward and ungainly items to pack, carry and store. A mass of struts and frames, levers and pins are nothing but a nuisance. It is often not fully appreciated that they generally only support quite a light weight and have to do little more than keep the railway some distance above the floor. I have taken the easiest possible course, each leg being just a separate post held vertical by a strut and placed along the layout in a piggyback fashion (*Fig. 21*). The first board has four legs and all the others merely two.

Each post is a length of 2 in. x 1 in. pine and the strut a strip of 2 in. x ¼ in. parana pine (*Fig. 21a*). The position of the two bolt holes and the screw around which the strut pivots, can be found out by trial and error or triangulation, that is, making the distance between their centres form a right-angled triangle, and keeping their lengths in the ratio of 5:4:3 (Pythagoras theorem) (*Fig. 21b*). The bolts are 6 mm diameter guttering bolts which can be purchased 80 mm long with matching wing nuts from a builder's yard. I drilled holes in the frames of the baseboard and screwed each bolt in so that it tapped itself into the wood. Another lesson learnt over the years is not to have too many loose bolts. The legs are held firmly in place by the wing nuts.

I hope that by following the simple principles that I have outlined, you can saw, hammer and glue with the confidence that the resulting baseboards will be successful, reliable, and easily achieved.

A level trackbed, but also one that captures accurately and perceptively the variations of the prototype.

TRACKLAYING

From the days of the Stockton and Darlington Railway, a level and well drained trackbed was vital for the safe operation of the fastest express or slowest pick-up goods. Track was laid in a bed of ballast whether granite, limestone or ash, and levelled by tamping this under the sleepers. The same care is needed in laying and aligning a level trackbed on our model, but we achieve this in a very different way.

It would be foolish to expect our models to run smoothly and without derailments unless the track was flat. As we cannot tamp ballast under the sleepers the best way of achieving level track is to glue it to a flat baseboard. This has been emphasised in the past few pages, as the design and construction of the baseboard is the key to reliable, trouble-free running, and the techniques I have described have proved themselves to be extremely successful not only for myself, but for others who have adopted this system.

I don't believe that any form of rubber or sponge laid beneath the track will

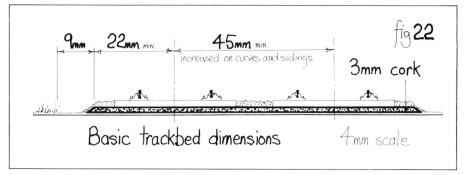

compensate for bad carpentry, but on most open track some kind of base is needed to suggest the appearance of the ballast shoulder (*Fig. 22*). I much prefer 3mm thick cork floor tiles as this high quality material comes flat and can be cut and shaped easily. It is often suggested that a rubber base under the track will give quieter running, but in my experience this advantage is soon lost when ballast is glued over it.

Super elevation can be introduced into this bed of cork, but unless tilted with extreme accuracy and care, more problems are likely to arise. As this feature is more noticeable on lines away

from a station and never on curves as tight as ours, I would question whether the improvement in appearance is justified if reliable operation is at risk. However, look at photographs of the prototype first, and decide for yourself. Also study the appearance of the ballast as many a winding rural branch line, particularly in pre-grouping days, had a very flat undefined edge quite unlike the main lines of the 1980s with their high and more generous shouldered and chamfered edges.

I mark and cut out the cork with a craft knife, chamfering the edges, if needed, with a piece of glasspaper wrapped around a wooden block before gluing to the chipboard base. I have used PVA glue (Unibond), but find that it tends to make the cork curl up at its edges; a more appropriate glue is Unibond Contact Adhesive which can be applied with a brush as it is water-based and thus easy to spread.

Before track is laid I drill any holes for point motors and I always mark the ends of the rails where they cross the baseboard joint. It is here that there is a danger of the rails being ripped up accidentally so I prefer to solder the ends to small screws fastened into the board. Naturally once the screw is in place, its head can be slimmed down with a file so that its appearance is not noticeable.

Track and turnouts, whether Peco, Alan Gibson or homemade, can either be glued down in a thick bed of PVA glue and the ballast sprinkled on top, or fixed with a contact glue like Evostik and ballasted later. This second method of placing dry ballast between the sleepers and dropping a mix of PVA and water over the top has become very popular of late (*Fig. 23*). There is a danger with the first method of ending up with too much glue which can result in the ballast finishing above the sleeper tops. This is not just unprototypical but looks dreadful.

Diluting the PVA helps but great care and practice are still needed. The second method has the advantage of making wiring easier and track-laying becomes clearer without a covering of ballast in the way.

Perhaps the most effective method of securing dry ballast is to allow the spray from a plant mister to fall gently over the track until it is quite damp. Then a diluted mix of PVA (with a dash of washing-up liquid to eliminate meniscus effect) can be liberally applied with an eye dropper. The pre-dampened track tends to attract the glue down into the ballast. However, the glue tends to leave a slightly shiny appearance to the ballast,

and if granite is used it will turn to a bluish/green shade. This is unfortunate as the subtle range of colours and tones present in the natural stone will be lost as it will be necessary to apply a thin wash of paint to restore a more natural appearance. To my mind neither method is perfect, but I favour the latter method and proceed once all the scenery is painted; in that way the ballast will not be covered in green splashes.

So to summarise the order of track-laying as it fits into the story of landscape modelling: first cut and glue down the cork, second fix the track and lastly, once all the scenery is complete, ballast the track.

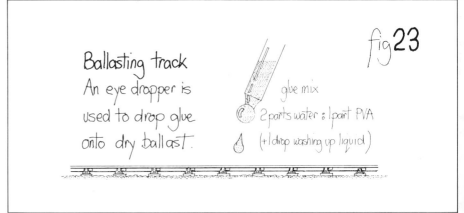

Ballasting track
An eye dropper is used to drop glue onto dry ballast.

fig 23

glue mix
2 parts water : 1 part PVA
(+ 1 drop washing up liquid)

Careful tracklaying and ballasting complete a trackbed that looks as if it is built through the surrounding land.

CHAPTER THREE

Foundations for a Landscape

CREATING A LANDSCAPE

Sheep scattered on a lonely hillside sheltering in the shadows of dry-stone walls, a binder grasping each sheaf of corn and throwing it towards a stubbled gently rolling patchwork of fields, or perhaps water lapping the banks of a slow and winding river beneath the parapet walls of a rusting girder bridge, are settings which may convey the kind of atmosphere that you wish to capture in miniature. We are about to tread towards achieving this.

In the same way that photographs and drawings guide the crafting of a convincing model of a locomotive made from brass and nickel silver, building a landscape should demand the same visual awareness — a familiarization with the prototype is essential. It is more convincing and often easier to copy details from real life than to fabricate features from the imagination. We may wonder how big a cornfield would be in Suffolk, or how wide the River Wye is, as it washes the banks of the meadowland neighbouring Tintern station. However, hopefully most of these questions will have been answered when designing and researching the layout. It is only once a good technical knowledge as well as an aesthetic appreciation of the landscape has been achieved, that a real start can be made.

The first requirement must be an estimation of the slope of bordering hillsides as this influences the basic landscape shell. However, beware! A hill that appears quite steep will, when measured, be much flatter than you had imagined (*Fig. 24a*). Thus it is often better to compensate for the illusion of distance with a little exaggeration (*Fig. 24b*). This can be of help when blending the 3-dimensional landscape into the 2-dimensional backscene, as it is a good idea to increase the slope of the land progressively as the two meet.

This distortion of perspective can be enhanced when adding details like hedges, buildings and trees in two ways, firstly, by moving together distant objects like hedges, and secondly by reducing the scale to which they are built (*Fig. 25*).

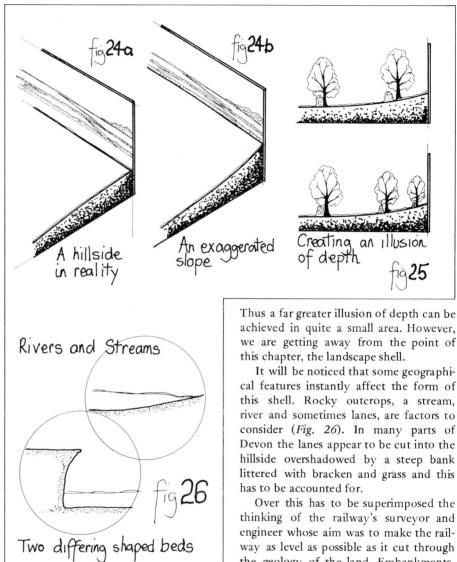

A hillside in reality

An exaggerated slope

Creating an illusion of depth

fig 24a

fig 24b

fig 25

Rivers and Streams

Two differing shaped beds

fig 26

fig 27

A logical view of how a railway is built

Thus a far greater illusion of depth can be achieved in quite a small area. However, we are getting away from the point of this chapter, the landscape shell.

It will be noticed that some geographical features instantly affect the form of this shell. Rocky outcrops, a stream, river and sometimes lanes, are factors to consider (*Fig. 26*). In many parts of Devon the lanes appear to be cut into the hillside overshadowed by a steep bank littered with bracken and grass and this has to be accounted for.

Over this has to be superimposed the thinking of the railway's surveyor and engineer whose aim was to make the railway as level as possible as it cut through the geology of the land. Embankments, bridges and cuttings were all constructed to realise this objective. Investigate these to estimate their size and shape, noting how they harmonise with the land around them. Think logically and avoid the mistake of making the railway look as if it was built first (*Fig. 27*). Imagine the flow of the land without the railway, and then see if the line appears to take a logically sweeping course over this.

Hopefully most of these ideas have already been mulled over earlier, and put to good effect in that essential exercise of building a miniature of the model.

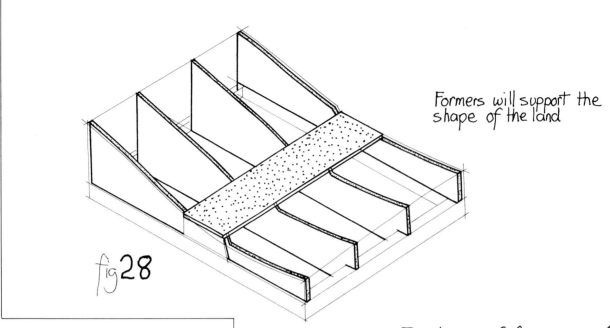

Formers will support the shape of the land

fig 28

BUILDING A STRUCTURE

Now this is really it — the start of those rolling hills, granite outcrops or chalk embankments. The basic idea is to cut formers to the profile of the land and then position them every 9″-12″ along the layout (*Fig. 28*). They will provide a contour upon which to lay a covering of chicken wire, and essentially form the shape of your landscape.

I use 12 mm thick, very cheap and soft insulation board because it can be cut so easily. It can also be easily corrected or altered with a Surform or glasspaper until it looks right (*Fig. 29*). You will in addition find that it slides into the base-board frame and is convenient to fit (*Fig. 30a & 30b*).

I start work in the middle of the lay-out, moving in both directions towards the ends. This first piece is the hardest, as it will dictate the general slope of all the others as they flow to meet it. I draw its profile out using the 3-D model as a guide, just scaling it up. It is cut out with a combination of different saws (tenon, hand, coping) and some old hack-saw blades. Once in place, it is carefully scrutinized and if need be its shape corrected with glasspaper or a Surform.

For the second profile it is easiest to draw round the first and then to alter it. Think about two things, the line of the horizon, or rather the join between the 3-dimensional shell and the backscene, and the slope to which the land is heading. For most models the change will be small,

Two types of former

fig 29

Insulation board

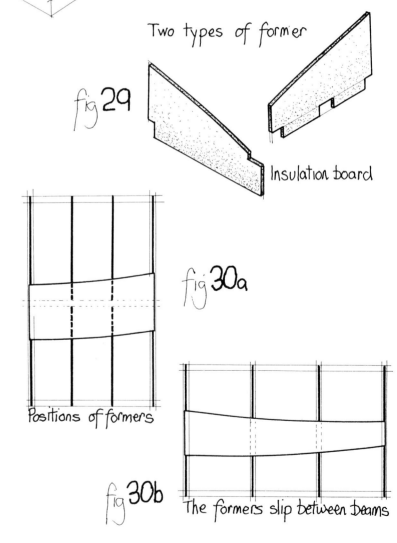

fig 30a

Positions of formers

fig 30b

The formers slip between beams

in some there may be little or no change at all.

It is quite common for the railway to hug a hillside and just twist and turn with it. It may slice through a ridge forming a cutting or arrive at another valley and have to cross it. All the time it is necessary to look at the real thing, the prototypical setting. This will tell you what direction you should be heading for, and if you pay attention to it, your model will be refreshingly real. Remember, do not try and make it all up, a hopeless unconvincing bit of countryside will result, showing no reason for its existence.

Gradually working along the layout, each profile board will tell you a little more about the next. Your eye is the best judge and most valuable tool. Look along the model from different angles, check that surface of the land rolls smoothly as it engulfs the railway.

Once the wooden supports for the land are in place, fill in the back and front edges with the same insulation board, making sure they produce a nice flowing line (*Fig. 31*). However, for a narrow baseboard less than 21 ins. it would be easier to reverse the process. Cut the front and back formers first out of 4mm ply and then fit in the profile board, still using insulation board (*Fig. 33*). Within this structure lie lanes and roads. These very ancient rights of way preceded the railway by many centuries. They must be made to appear as if they continue on their natural course, perhaps interrupted when crossing the railway on bridges or perhaps by a level crossing. Each lane needs a base and this is cut from insulation board and glued between the land profiles (*Fig. 32*). It may be necessary to route the lanes up hill and down dale, in which case any bends in the surface can be introduced by cutting half through the back of the material, and filling the cuts with glue (*Fig. 32a*). Similarly, rivers and streams are modelled on a base of insulation board that is best cut to a more generous width than the river bed. Upon this the banks and water's edges can be shaped and a useful material to do this is expanded polystyrene which is most conveniently purchased in the form of ceiling tiles that are glued together. A useful source of thicker 1 in. material is a cold water tank insulation kit which is really just five sheets of expanded polystyrene that fit together to make a box.

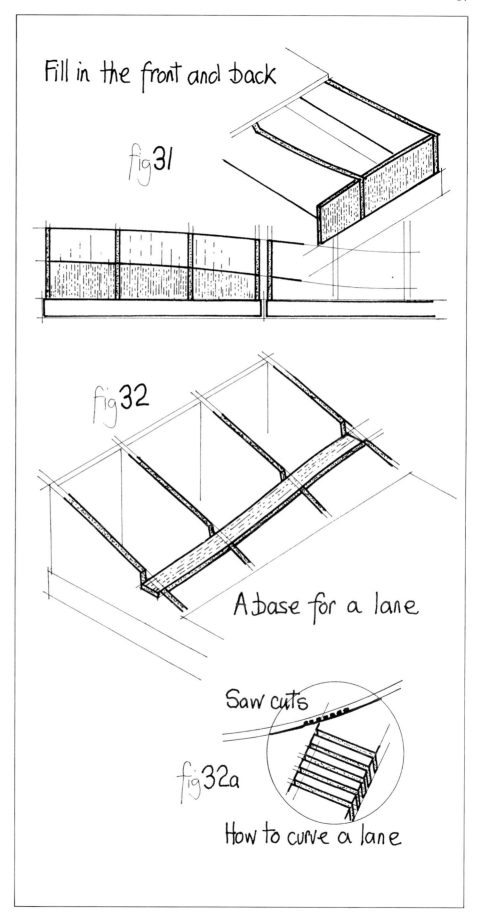

Fill in the front and back

fig 31

fig 32

A base for a lane

Saw cuts

fig 32a

How to curve a lane

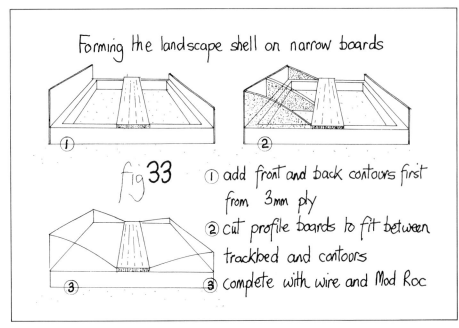

Forming the landscape shell on narrow boards

Fig 33

① add front and back contours first from 3mm ply

② cut profile boards to fit between trackbed and contours

③ complete with wire and Mod Roc

This material is very useful for small areas of embankment or hillside, where the process of cutting formers and stretching a skin over them is too involved. It is wise to look and think about the easiest ways of forming the slope of the land; broadly speaking, polystyrene is useful for small areas to a maximum width of about 75 mm, and the cutting of formers for the remainder of land. Details like rocky outcrops and river banks need to make use of the properties of polystyrene into which a basic strata can be carved. Although this material is best cut with a hot wire cutter, I see little point in buying one, unless a great deal of use is to be made of this material. I find it easier to slice and carve using a hacksaw blade or old breadknife (a new one if you can smuggle one from the kitchen). Finishing details fall to the abrasion of glass paper, or rasps, and a vacuum cleaner will clean up the unfortunate mess.

It is pleasant to step back and look at the model in this state. The railway will begin to look as if it is part of the surroundings, lost amidst hills and valleys. I'm sure you will get that satisfied feeling of achieving realism, for this is where real prototype atmosphere begins.

SURFACE COVERING

The next step is simple, the time when the skeleton begins to have its skin replaced. I use chicken wire to cover the formers, for there is no better material (*Fig. 34*). It can be purchased in a number of different mesh sizes, the smallest ½ in. being the most suited to our needs. The width varies as well, but try to get a size that will cover the whole of the hillside, from trackbed to backscene. To stretch over the Cornish hills of Petherick I needed the widest I could find – 24 ins.

You will immediately see the advantage of having a portable layout, or at least one that falls into sections. I like to move a board at a time on to an old table and work on it there. It is easier to be able to walk all around the board when stapling the chicken wire in place. I start by cutting a piece approximately 2 inches longer and wider than the area to be covered, taking care not to fold or crease it. The idea is to lay it down, stapling it into position and then to fold the edges over by about 1 inch. However, beware, this can be a vicious material and, being rolled, it particularly likes to pounce and claw itself over your hands, so be careful.

If you haven't got a staple gun, you will find it a very useful and worthwhile tool to acquire. Starting from one end, I staple down along each profile board, pulling the wire taut all the time. Not surprisingly, the staples will not hold themselves very tightly on the edges of these boards and it is only once the overlap at the ends and side are folded over and stapled that it becomes secure (*Fig. 35*). The join with the trackbed will provide a further anchor if stapled into the chipboard every 2 inches. This is an area where only a staple gun will do, a normal paper stapler just hasn't got the power needed.

If a road or riverbed inhibits the flow of the wire, cut into it and fold it to a realistic edge before stapling again (*Fig. 36*). The more diverse geological features are set into the model by twisting, folding or cutting the wire where appropriate. Take care to mould it around rocks, thinking about how nature does it, this can be your only true guide.

Laying down a hard skin is the final step. I use Mod Roc plaster bandage, but the same results could be achieved with plasterers' scrim and plaster. If you ever read the instructions on the packet of Mod Roc and follow them, I'm sure that you will only end up with a tangled mess

of soggy crumpled bandage. I find it much easier to lay it dry, before painting on the water. Roll out the bandage down the hillside and start painting on the water with a 2 in. wide brush. Take the next piece and half overlap the first before painting it with water. The size of the overlap can be reduced on narrower hillsides. (*Fig. 37*). Continue this process across the board, remembering to fold down the edges at the back and ends, securing them well with water. Work fast as the plaster goes off in about 10 minutes and cannot be resoftened.

To give the surface a drum-like quality, it needs to be strengthened. I was a little disappointed with the lack of rigidity in the skin and searched for a way of gaining a tough shell. In fact the way to achieve this is surprisingly easy and effective. It is simply a matter of plastering underneath to fill the gaps between the mesh of the chicken wire (*Fig. 38*). This prevents the wire from compressing, holding it in tension. Only a very thin layer is needed, perhaps only 1 mm to 1½ mm thick, and should leave the surface of the wire showing once it is painted on.

I was going to use dental plaster; however, living in a village community, tracking down a dental supplier proved difficult. As an alternative, Polyfilla mixed with PVA glue is spread between the wire. I expected to use numerous packets of Polyfilla but was surprised how far it went. If you haven't added

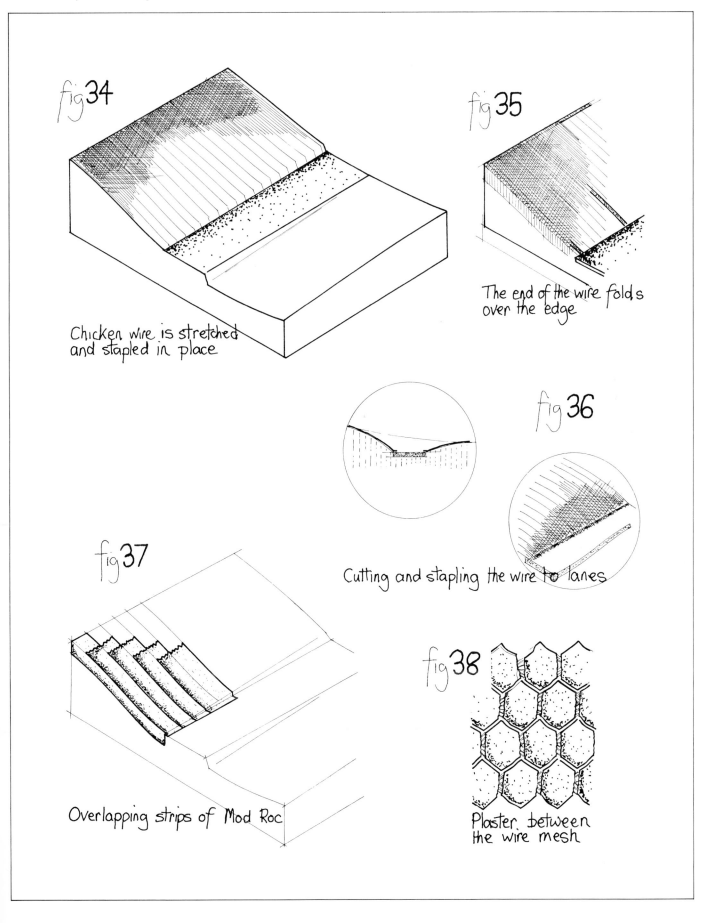

fig 34

Chicken wire is stretched
and stapled in place

fig 35

The end of the wire folds
over the edge

fig 36

Cutting and stapling the wire to lanes

fig 37

Overlapping strips of Mod Roc

fig 38

Plaster between
the wire mesh

A sneaky view of the formers that support the landscape shell of chicken wire and plaster bandage.

Unibond PVA to a mix before, you will find that a spoonful will take the brittleness out of the plaster, giving it a slightly plastic quality.

Before we can sit back and think about planting grass, there is just one last finishing process. It is necessary to seal the surface to prevent it from flaking and give it a textured base for all detail work (*Fig. 39*). Rather than developing an earth mix with sand, sawdust and plaster, I looked for something simpler. A most successful solution is achieved by using textured paint such as Marleytex or Supatex which are available from DIY shops and is meant to be used for texturing ceilings and walls. If you peer into the tub it looks like paint mixed with grit or sand. Painting this with a 1½ inch paint brush over the whole layout will give a tough pliable and textured surface to the Mod Roc.

As the last brush stroke dries, we rest at another completed stage. The shimmer of rails now reflects the white wintry bleakness of its surroundings and it is time to set about detailing.

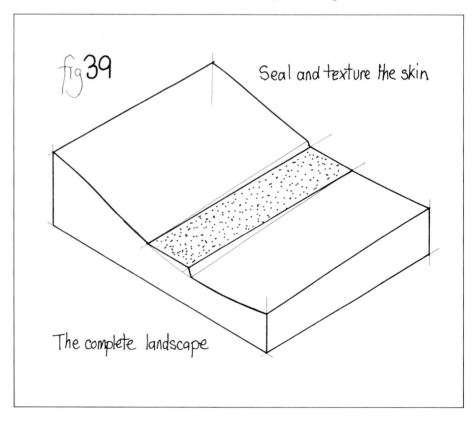

fig 39

Seal and texture the skin

The complete landscape

Chicken wire is stapled to the chipboard trackbase.

The wire is folded over the front and back edges.

Mod-Roc plaster bandage places a skin over the wire.

The underside is lightly plastered, resulting in a tough shell.

A textured paint is brushed over the surface to both seal and texture it. Marleytex is one example of a suitable gritty paint.

Edwardian North Cornwall – just as I imagine it to have been.

Rosebay willow herb and nettles grow tangled with long tufted grass along the embankment.

CHAPTER FOUR

Detailing the Landscape

EMBANKMENTS AND CUTTINGS

These features form a convenient and satisfyingly easy point to start detailing, but unfortunately they are often modelled very badly. I first marked the full extent of the embankments i.e. to include railway land inside the boundary fence where the coarseness of the tufted grass contrasts with the apparently smooth appearance of the bordering pasture land.

The rather brilliant white of the plaster base needs to be toned down now so that the brightness is not reflected beneath the grass. I have not found it necessary to paint the surface dark brown, or even an earth colour, but just give it a wash of browness to tone down the base. I use Burnt Sienna powder paint mixed to a very watery consistency (*Fig. 40*). A large brush, about 1½ in. wide washes it quickly around the trackside and along the layout, colouring the ground before

we start thinking about the texture of the grass.

A glance at the prototype will generally show that these areas or strips of railway property create an impression of roughness, with clumps of grass drying at their

fig 40

Powder paint

A wash of Burnt Umber

ends in the hot summer sun, tangled with weeds, bracken and bushes. However, it is wise to look more closely at the area you are modelling as the nature of the soil or rock beneath will determine the richness and variety of the growth on top. I noticed that beside the track in Derbyshire the grass was quite fine as the scree or rock underneath didn't support much life. A scattering of broken rocks and stones showed through the grass and made the ground beneath more obvious. Conversely in the West Country, the damp warm climate, and rich soil, presented quite a different picture. The railway is bordered by flowing bracken, gorse, nettles and the fiery pink and purple of the Rosebay Willow herb. Filled with this empathy for the location of the model, we can set about trying to capture the atmosphere, character and uniqueness of our favoured area in our model making.

I tried many things to capture that dried long grass appearance, and it soon became clear that only through using carpet underfelt could I make a realistic impression of the scene. Found in most old houses, this is a dark brown colour, about 6 mm thick and has a coarse and hairy texture. This is also available in a roll for sound-proofing the body shell of a car. A DIY motor accessory shop will sell two types. I find the one without a thin rubber backing the better.

To begin with it needs to be bleached. This will remove the brown dye so that it can be painted to give an authentic parched summery look. I have tried painting the felt while it is still brown, but it just didn't work for me. Bleaching it will give you an attractive and versatile beige colour to work from and by adding a couple of cups of bleach to a washing up bowl half full of water, a night's soaking will remove all the colour. It is important to pull the felt apart beforehand so that the bleach will fully penetrate (*Fig. 41*).

To lay or plant the felt, brush the embankment or area to be covered with a fairly generous layer of PVA glue. I always use the same 1½ inch brush and as cheap a PVA as I can find, such as Berol Marvin Medium or Unibond. Into this bed of glue I push small wads or ½ inch diameter 'balls' of bleached felt, pressing down far more pieces than appears to be necessary, to make a thick covering.

Once dry, pinch the felt and pull it off in wads. This pinching effect will leave clumps of grass, but be prepared to pull off more than you think you ought to (*Fig. 42*). Remember to look at the prototype, you may find your embank-

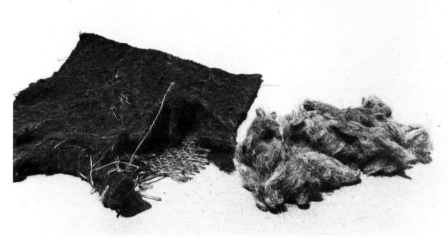

Carpet underfelt, pulled apart and ready to be bleached.

fig 41

The carpet felt is split in half then torn into wads

Bleach + water

Wads of bleached felt are pinched off to leave the clumped effect of long grass.

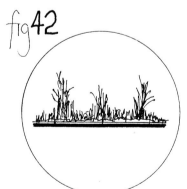

fig 42

The clumped effect

The play of light unfolds a variety of textures and colours, capturing the rugged nature of a lineside cutting.

ment should look very thin in patches, so use your eyes and observe the real thing.

Colour brings life and interest to a model and here I wanted to capture the effect of the rich green grass at the roots of the embankment, that gradually fade to a pale straw tint at their tips. I have always found water colours the easiest medium to work with. By applying washes of colour, and changing the shade of the mix, a sympathetic and subtle variation of hue and tone results. Just as an artist uses the whiteness of his paper to show through his washes of colour,

we look to the base colour of the bleached felt for a similar effect. It is important to be aware that colouring *must* be done under the lighting conditions that the model will normally be seen by. A dull day, bright sunlight, fluorescent lights and tungsten lighting will all make different demands upon the balance of colour. Petherick was built and painted under tungsten lighting (spot lights); the colours look too yellow under fluorescent tubes and on a dull day, but good in bright sun. Controlling the play of light is very much a problem with an exhibition layout unless it can be boxed in with a roof.

I make a mix of 3 dabs of Sap Green, 1 dab of Hooker Green Dark, a little Burnt Sienna and between 4 and 6 teaspoonsful of water. I prefer Winsor & Newton Artists water colour, Cotman range, in a tube (*Fig. 43*). Beware that the same named colour will vary between different manufacturers' paint, its pigment may be more intense and not compatible with another maker's range. Water colour is also by way of its nature, differing in permanence. Some colours will be more

permanent than others and not so prone to fading in sunlight. A chart is available from an artists' materials stockist that will tell you clearly which colours are the most fugitive. Having said that, Sap Green is not the most permanent, but just how long it will retain its full colour I wouldn't like to say. This will depend on the amount of daylight a model receives but I should think that most models will have seen the end of their days long before the colours fade.

The small mix of colour described may seem inadequate, but it goes a long way, and by making numerous mixes there is always a subtle yet desirable variation in the colour.

To make the paint flow through the long grass I add a tiny drop of washing-up liquid to every mix; this will break down the surface tension of the water. Again all the painting is done with a 1½ inch brush, leaving the embankment very wet and soggy. Once dry, the hairs of the felt can be lifted by brushing with a nailbrush.

Nothing looks more unnatural than the whole embankment looking the same

Contrasting textures between the embankment and meadow.

texture. The green base needs detailing to bring it alive, so think back to those shrubs, weeds and bushes that are characteristic of the line being modelled. Ferns in the Forest of Dean, bright golden gorse in Norfolk, or perhaps a blaze of purple Rose Bay Willow herb sweeping across a cutting.

With a selection of lichen, moss and both Woodland Scenic flock and mat laid out on a handy table or bench, detailing can begin. Lichen forms the base of bushes; by taking small lumps and holding them in an old pair of tweezers, they can be sprayed with photomount glue (*Fig. 44*). It is worth mentioning that Scotch make three types of spray glue,

'Photomount' in a red tin, 'Spray Mount' in a blue tin and 'Display Mount' in a brown tin, the latter being the strongest and most suitable for our needs. They are then shaken in a tub of minced up foam flock powder, like the Woodland Scenics coarse turf range. The glue really penetrates the fibres of the lichen, forming a light and delicate bush.

The same approach, using a piece of rubberized horsehair, produces a slightly more coarse bush, and an excellent base for gorse. The medium green flock blends well with the coloured embankment, but for the darker more blue hue of brambles a darker green flock powder is obviously better. Look for the patterns made by the wild growth over the grass, a large mass of bushes is more effective than a lot of smaller groups. For the smallest of details like the scattering of low lying plants, I simply cut holes in a piece of thin card,

Spray with Glue

fig 44

A bush of lichen

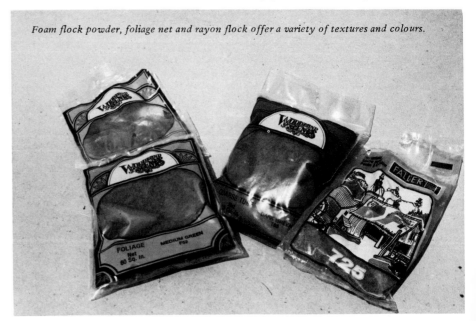

Foam flock powder, foliage net and rayon flock offer a variety of textures and colours.

place it on the grass and spray through the holes with glue. This will restrict the adhesive to small areas that can be sprinkled with flock.

To break the ground cover up with another texture, sisal string and jute are very handy. Jute is much finer than sisal, and can be bought as a twine, used normally for making hanging baskets. I cut this to a length of about 12mm, dip the end in PVA glue, and stand it on an embankment in small or large clumps. With a touch of rusty coloured paint and surrounding tissue leaves, it represents docks, or with a dab of glue and a sprinkling of flock it will capture nettles.

Single strands of sisal can also form the stems of wild flowers. By adding a dab of yellow for Ragwort or perhaps

white, red or blue to the ends, an impression of colour and texture is soon built up (*Fig. 45*). When colouring flowers, water or oil paint never really gives a vividness to the colours. To avoid a rather dull and lifeless appearance, it is worth buying a few cheap fluorescent water colours to add a sparkle to the flora.

Large plants like Rose Bay Willow Herb will have to be modelled individually.

The main stem is cut from a hard bristle brush, and each bristle systematically dipped in PVA glue and then flock powder (*Fig. 46*). Once dry, a lick of purple paint, and a trim to length, completes it ready for planting. Don't forget that stones and rocks may form an equally

A hard bristle brush

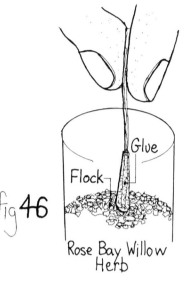

fig 45

Simple wild flowers

fig 46

Glue

Flock

Rose Bay Willow Herb

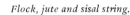

Flock, jute and sisal string.

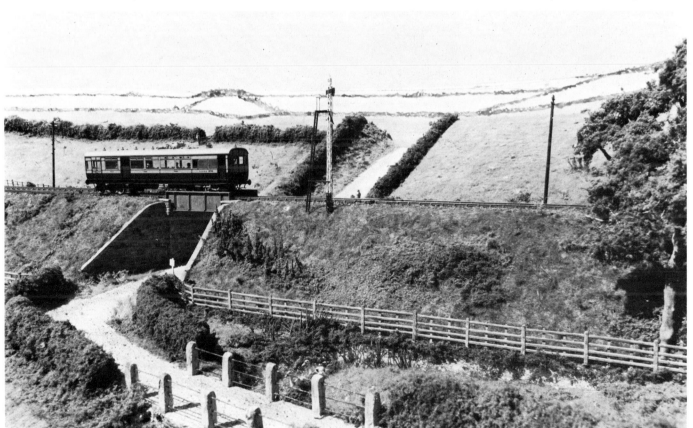

Simply made weeds and flowers add detail and interest to an embankment.

important feature, not to be missed, but that's another subject outside the intended scope of this book.

I have always found this kind of detailing interesting and relaxing. I like experimenting with different materials and looking for interesting topics to model. It is important not to lose sight of the prototype, and best to consider what you perceive in terms of its patterns, textures and colours.

PASTURES AND MEADOWS

With such an expanse of green surrounding Petherick, it was important to create variety and interest in every field. Cattle contentedly graze in a meadow carpeted with buttercups and daisies and elsewhere sheep are scattered over a hillside, dotted by thistles, scarred by a tangle of nettles, and the rusty heads of the dock. However, before thinking too much about the differences between individual meadows, we need a basic grass texture to detail.

Grass appears very fine and grows unevenly in clumps. Add to this the effects of weather, grazing and harvesting, and a whole range of interesting subjects are there to be modelled. But what should be used as a base? I have tried scatters of both the ground foam and sawdust types but these appear too coarse and seem more suited to detailing work. I also tried rayon flock which is more of the fibrous nature of grass, but again this appears too coarse and uniform in texture. My choice is normal surgical lint that can be bought from a chemist (*Fig. 47*). If this is laid so that the material backing can be removed, the fibres left can then be teased with a brush and a very convincing impression of pastures and meadows can be built up on this base.

However, before any attempt is made to glue lint in place, the white ground surface needs colouring. This may well vary from place to place. Look at the rich red soil in Devon around Exeter, or the whiteness of the chalk hills in Wiltshire. This base colour will show through the grass, albeit subtly, so it needs to be considered carefully, as it will be an important factor in inducing the right atmosphere. I put down a thin wash of Burnt Sienna powder colour, in the same way that I did when preparing the embankments and cuttings. Remember that we are watercolour artists applying washes of colour, so don't use thick bold colours, they will be too dominant.

Cattle graze amongst a meadow of buttercups.

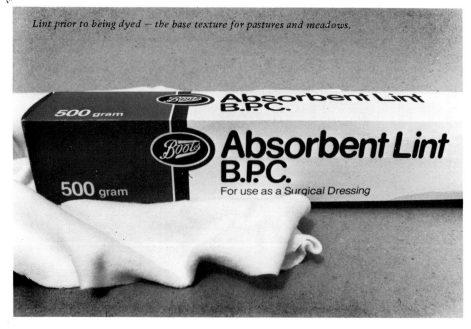

Lint prior to being dyed — the base texture for pastures and meadows.

Cut hay dries in the sun while sheep roam the hillside, just two effects built upon a bed of lint.

I can't deny that it is easier to put down glue and sprinkle on flock powders, but the difference achieved in using lint is amazing. It is not difficult to apply although it is wise to practise first. Again I use PVA glue, not the Thixofix type often recommended. This is probably just the opposite advice given by everyone else who has used this technique, but perhaps not to the extent that I have. Thixofix is very expensive and I found it difficult to spread over a texture surface, and I also found that it tends to colour the ground surface sometimes, making it shiny. It proved so much easier, cheaper and reliable to use PVA on Petherick that where I had used both I ended up scrubbing off all the areas fixed with Thixofix and refixing the lint with PVA.

The secret of success is to lay down a very thin layer of glue and I mean *thin*. Squeeze it from the brush so that the surface is covered with glue, but not very wet, and of course not dry. An old 1½ inch paint brush with worn stubbly hairs

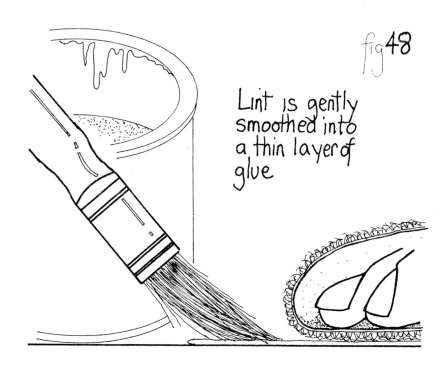

fig 48

Lint is gently smoothed into a thin layer of glue

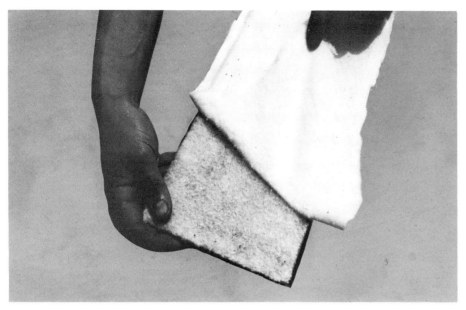

The lint backing is ripped off, leaving a fine covering of hairs upon the ground (lint undyed).

a lush pasture effect. With a dry summer, the land appears more parched and this colouring can be introduced later by using an airbrush to spray Cadmium Yellow and Burnt Umber onto the tips of the grass. An overall bareness is only apparent when the grass has been cut or grazed short, after which it soon dries under the hot sun.

The texture of grass

is ideal. Only paint the glue over a small area, a strip about 150 mm wide, before smoothing down the lint with its hairs in the glue (*Fig. 48*). I start gluing at one edge of each board, laying the glue in strips and rolling down the lint.

The next day the backing can be removed by pulling up a corner and tugging it off. This is one of my favourite stages, a satisfying rip as the hairs get left on the hillside. You should be able to see the colour of the ground through the lint, but only just, and not too much. If the backing does not pull off, it will probably have soaked up the glue, and then you really do have problems. If this happens you will have to slide a knife blade between the backing and ground, and gently slice your way through the hairs of the lint. Too little glue causes the lint to appear too thin but this can be remedied by repeating the process. One final point must be stressed, remember that the surface to which the lint is laid must be sealed, in our case with textured paint, otherwise when ripping off the lint backing, the ground surface will come with it.

Although the surface is fairly even, this will be roughened up during the painting stage, again using Artists Watercolours applied with a brush. It should be mentioned that the most authentic grass colour is achieved if the lint is dyed first. Follow the instructions on a tin of Dylon Olive Green (No. 34) and this will provide a base colour on which to wash the water colour. To my standard mix of Sap

Green, Hooker Green, Dark and Burnt Sienna, I now add 8 teaspoonsful of water. If I vary the amount of Dark Hooker Green and reduce the quantity of Burnt Sienna (*Fig. 49*), this puts a little more blue into the green, producing quite

During painting it is disappointing to see all the fine hairs of the lint lying flat and soggy, but this will dry and can be used to good effect. Remember that we are looking for a clumped appearance (*Fig. 50*), a variety in textures between the smooth and rugged. To introduce this a nailbrush is an essential tool. By pushing it into the dry flattened lint, and moving it from side to side, the hairs will be lifted. I tend to put the brush down, rub from side to side and lift it, move a little, put it down, and again move it from side to side. In this way the surface is lifted in clumps and an uneven

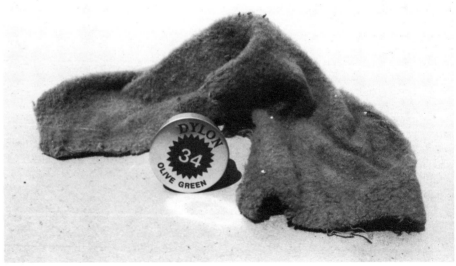

The white lint has to be dyed green before it can be used effectively.

texture can be controlled. After covering the whole field like this, step back and check to see if any more needs scrubbing to produce the effect that lingers in your mind. Remember that what you have here is a base ready for detailing, a point from which different fields can be modelled.

'Why are fields different?', you may ask; they are, after all, just a bed of grass! The differences arise mainly through the grazing of different animals, and the need to harvest hay and silage. If you look at a field well eaten by sheep, it will appear much shorter and smoother than the same field grazed by cattle. The movement of animals from one pasture to another allows new growth to flourish whilst it is left fallow. Animals also have little liking for thistles, nettles and docks; these you will see celebrating their victory over the attacking cattle. Plants such as buttercups and daisies soon spring up and flower, tending to struggle to the surface when left alone by the wandering beasts. Naturally climate is another factor which changes a rather tired and parched grassland into a rich green pasture. Water collects at the foothills and in meadows, giving quite a different appearance, a far more lush environment than unsheltered or rocky hillsides.

The growth of hay is an interesting study. The long grass, sometimes a pale purple at its seed head, sways in the summer breeze amongst the thistles and buttercups. It is cut and starts to dry in the sun with the farmer turning it every so often, until it is dry enough to be

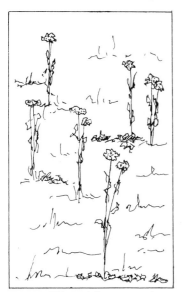

Thistles *fig* **52**

Paint will flatten the hairs of the lint but they can be teased up again with a nailbrush.

Spray glue through template

fig 53

stored. I always think that it is a most spectacular sight, when new vivid and sometimes fluorescent green shoots come to life beneath the drying cut hay. This is such a contrast to the relative dullness of the surrounding fields. Go and look, see for yourself so that you can capture the atmosphere in your modelling.

A grazed field is rich in thistles (*Fig. 52*). These I produce from sisal string, cutting a small bunch of about three or four strands, 12 mm - 16 mm long, that are then glued to the field. When they are stuck, a dab of PVA on the top and sides is followed by a sprinkle of flock powder. A wash of pale green paint, and their heads dotted with purple captures their appearance.

Neighbouring nettles are tackled in two ways, a low covering is represented by Woodland Scenics coarse turf foam glued down in small patches on the grass.

This I found is best achieved by spraying Display Mount glue in a controlled application on to the grass. I usually cut templates, just holes in a thin piece of card, and spray the glue through them before dabbing down the flock (*Fig. 53*). A similar technique is used on embankments where a template cut with a jagged edge is used to control the area of sprayed glue. This will allow the variety of small shrubs and weeds to be applied discriminately onto the surface of the long clumped grass. The taller nettles, straight and spikey, start with a core of

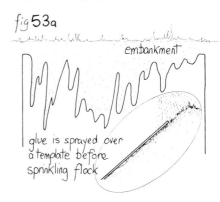

fig 53a

embankment

glue is sprayed over a template before sprinkling flock

sisal string. This is glued down in large clumps, a few strands at a time. With a variation in height and spacing, interesting groups can be formed to capture the texture and pattern of those painful stingers (*Fig. 54*). The dark green leaves are added once the string is dry, with a quick spray of Photomount and a sprinkling of flock.

Sometimes a field can be covered in docks, a surprising amount can grow

The station nestles beneath a patchwork of fields.

together. Again sisal, about three strands in a group, is glued in place, and the pattern repeated over, perhaps, a corner of a field. These can be leafed with small pieces of tissue paper or elaborated with Woodland Scenics scatter, but what then

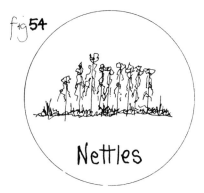

makes them look particularly interesting is that rich rusty colour, contrasting with the green of the grass. Of course you would have to be modelling late summer, but the effect is fascinating.

On to the base of the field beneath the grass I dotted buttercups and daisies. To obtain the fineness of the flowers, I used a pin rather than a brush as this will not apply the concentrated watercolour paint clearly. It was dipped in the thick yellow or white paint before stabbing the ground. This produces one of those subtle effects that may not be readily noticed, yet if it is not there it is sorely missed.

Another useful material is jute, a very fine natural beige twine ideal for adding long grass that has grown and turned to seed. It would be interesting to cover a whole field like this, but my patience has, as yet, not stretched that far. A quicker

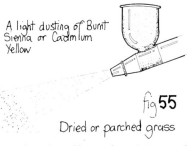

way to give the effect of seeded grass is to give the hillside a sweep of cadmium yellow from an airbrush (*Fig. 55*). Purple could be substituted for yellow, and as mentioned earlier, a fine mist of brown would look like parched land.

Of course the scope for further detailing is endless, but a combination of these techniques in differing ways will set your

Rain-beaten corn stands awaiting harvest.

model apart from others. Try to analyse the effects your are looking for, but again this can only be achieved by venturing out into the countryside and noting down what you see.

HAY, CORN AND BARLEY

Although I have fought shy of attempting to create a hayfield before it is cut, it can be modelled very easily after it is harvested. I turned to plumbers hemp which in many ways resembles the fineness of jute. It is purchased in a thick spine and I cut off a number of bundles about 12 mm long, separating the strands a little. These are glued down in a line across the field, but they must look as if they have been tossed about a little. The only way to appreciate the patterns made as the hay is cut, is once again to go in mid-July and look for yourself. By masking to leave a line, glue can be sprayed where it is needed, and the bed of chopped up hemp spread over it. To create more texture, I spread another layer on top of the first, after it had been sprayed with Display Mount. A field such as this could

come to life with a farmer tossing the hay with his pitchfork or horse-drawn hay tedder.

Man in his earliest of days fed himself by hunting the animals that roamed in our extensive forests. However, in his inventiveness he soon found that land could be cleared and crops raised. This gave him the capacity to produce more food and support a larger population. It is probably true that this trend has continued up to the present day but with scientific advance it is sometimes frightening to look out over a field of wheat or barley and to see every seed growing to the same height, and every square inch filled with grain. No doubt this perfection is a sign of our present technical achievements, but for the retrospective model maker it is wise to consider that in years past this was not the scene. I doubt whether a field of standing corn in 1910 would have the same regular appearance; it certainly would have been taller than strains grown today. The point I am making is that our landscape is subject to constant change and with farming a certain amount of

Plumbers hemp

historical research is needed to get simple details correct. Some of the more obvious differences in pre-war farming are highlighted in a very interesting article by Tim Watson which appeared in *Model Railway Journal* No. 10. This is well worth reading and should help many modellers to appreciate what they should aim for to be authentic.

The basis of my Edwardian field of standing corn is plumbers hemp. I first cut it into bundles about 16 mm long with a good sharp pair of scissors. A thick layer of PVA (about 1.5 mm) is spread onto the field and the bundles of hemp are planted side by side in it. It is not

The railway intrudes upon the tranquillity of hay-making at Little Missenden in 1934.

such a time consuming task as many would believe, a couple of evenings work will complete a good sized field. While gluing each bundle in position think of effects that can be modelled to reduce the uniformity of the crop. As mentioned, it should be thinned out, and in places it should be a little shorter where the quality of the land is poor or even water-logged. The most interesting effect is the devastation caused by heavy rain and gales, when large areas of corn are beaten down. Experiment here, by squashing it down with your finger (*Fig. 56*). However, avoid lots of small flattened areas as this generally occurs in large patches.

On to this swaying crop more subtle details can be introduced. Colour is perhaps the first. We all know that corn is yellow and grass is green, but nature is just a little more elusive than that. The colour of corn changes as it ripens. The natural colour of the hemp is near to the colour of wheat or barley just as it is about to be harvested, but in the previous weeks it will have turned from a golden yellow to a paler shade. Also growing with the corn would be poppies, corn-

flowers, grass and weeds, creating more colour. I used a leather punch to cut discs of red paper (rather oversize I might add) to copy the brightness and blaze of the poppy. Dabs of purple blue for corn-flowers and a sprinkling of green flock onto a spray of photomount for all the grass and weeds.

A corn field

Plumbers hemp stands in a thick layer of glue

fig 56

Of course, there are many more interesting and challenging scenes to model like a field of barley being cut by a horse-drawn reaper or a field of stooked corn, stacked for the prevailing winds to whistle past, or even the blackness of burnt stubble smouldering on the land. Always be aware of inconsistencies in seasonal growth, and the changes that have taken place with modern methods of farming. Today the combined harvester is followed by the bailer and then the plough, but a few years ago the scene was quite different and what now takes a week would have taken months, with ploughing in winter and threshing well into autumn. Again, for more information see Tim Watson's article.

Look for other crops that may be typical of the area which you are modelling — potatoes, beans, hops or today's bright fluorescent yellow rape in May. Experiment to get the textures, patterns and colours correct, but be wary of making a scene appear unnatural, and think about the balance between the amount of arable farming and livestock. This whole scene can soon become so interesting that you may even wonder why you bother to build a railway at all. In planning future projects I am now finding it difficult to fit the railway in with the rest of my ambition to capture the beauty of our homeland.

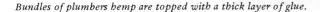

Bundles of plumbers hemp are topped with a thick layer of glue.

Poppies, rather overscale, are punched from scarlet paper.

A stand of elms and ash.

TREES

Trees tower over any gentle landscape, providing a home for birds, and shelter from prevailing winds. There can be few scenes that don't include a tree, so their stately presence really ought to feature on nearly any model. Again regional and even historic differences should be taken into consideration so first take a look at the scene. There can be the world of difference between the dense deciduous woodland of the Forest of Dean, for instance, and the towering elms of Constable country, or the closely packed shelter belts of Derbyshire. The types and way in which trees grow or appear to be grouped on a landscape, are important to consider if an authentic atmosphere is to be captured. There is so much difference in character between lanes winding by a spinney or shadowed by avenues of elms, and the cold and barren wilderness of moorland, where winds leave little

opportunity for the young saplings to establish themselves.

Look to see if certain species are more common than others and how they contribute to the unique character of any distinctive landscape. The scrubland of the Brecklands, that piece of Norfolk and Suffolk borderland, is endowed with Scots pines, their red barks scratched by gorse and bracken in the sandy soil, whilst Constable's immortal elms are inseparable from our image of the Stour Valley. Once again look for yourself and see how trees influence the atmosphere of your chosen landscape.

The only way to make a tree is to have a photograph or drawing to follow (*Fig. 58*). If you just make it up it is most unlikely to convince anyone. A good book to have beside you is the Ladybird 'Book of Trees' which features silhouettes of many types of British tree. It will show you the difference in shape between an

ash, elm or oak. If you decide to build, say, an elm, the next question is how big to make it. A fully grown tree will be some 50 cm high in 4 mm scale, impressive but perhaps too big. Don't be afraid to make large trees, you will find that they are easier to construct and more realistic. I made some elms and chose to keep them at about half their full size. I then looked for the main branches that would capture their shape, and made a simple drawing before starting.

There has been much written about making trees, and I would particularly recommend Bob Barlow's exquisite winter scenes described in *British Railway Journal* No. 3. However, I am going to summarise the methods I use, which although much simpler and quicker, are not as detailed.

For trunks and branches I use a very soft iron wire that is sold for making fences. It is 3 mm in diameter, made up

fig 58

Beech

Ash

Willow

Alder

Oak

Elm

Horse Chestnut

A play of sunlight through the boughs of an elm highlights its imposing size upon the landscape.

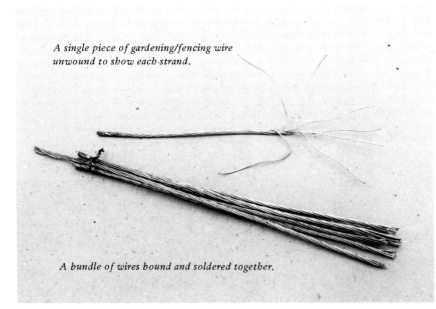

A single piece of gardening/fencing wire unwound to show each strand.

A bundle of wires bound and soldered together.

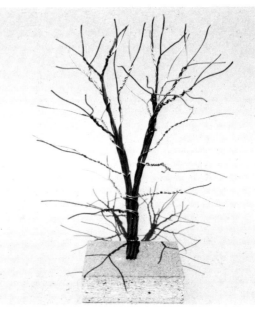

A framework of twisted branches.

of seven twisted strands, and can be purchased from an ironmongers. Depending on the tree, I cut either five or seven pieces a little longer than the full height of the tree. These are then bundled together and a loop of wire tied around their base (*Fig. 59*). This loop serves two purposes, it will hold the bundle tightly together, and provide an anchor to which each wire can be soldered. The soldering is easily performed with a blow torch, and plenty of flux, feeding the solder quickly around the loop. The middle

piece of wire is left longer to form a peg for securing the finished tree. Once the assembly has cooled down I set about twisting and untwisting the wires until they form the main structure of the tree (*Fig. 60*). It may be necessary to spot solder any loose branches or add further pieces of wire. Using this wire you will not have the fine branches and twigs that can be achieved using bowden or aircraft control cable, but for a tree with summer foliage this does not matter.

Over the years I have tried many materials to cover the wire and texture

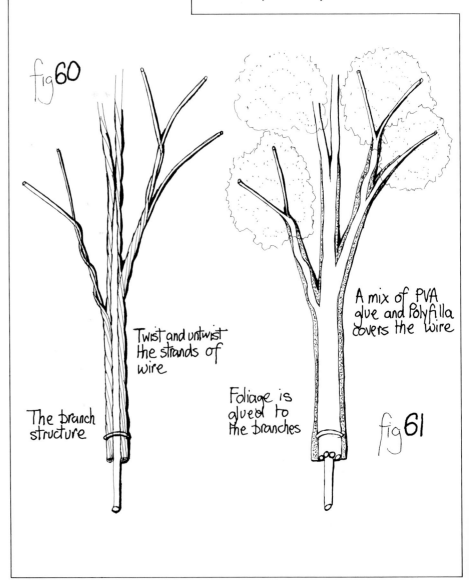

the bark. Once I used the parcel tape recommended by the legendary George Iliffe Stokes but I found this a horribly fiddly method and now I prefer plaster. The only problem with this is its inherent brittleness and tendency to crack off if the malleable wire framework of branches is knocked. To overcome this I add PVA glue to a mix of Polyfilla, which allows some flexibility when the plaster is dry. This mix can be painted over the wire with a brush and textured by dabbing on more of the mix as the first coat begins to dry (*Fig. 61*).

I use the Humbrol range of oil paints to colour the bark. If you study any local trees you will find they rarely appear brown but more likely grey. Rain will make them darker, so the colour can change from day to day, but remember that not all trees will have the same colour bark. Scots pines have an orange/red bark, whereas maturing silver birch are, of course, well known for their whitish appearance. It is wise to introduce a range of tones in the colouring of each tree, light grey, dark grey, a little brown and, of course, green for moss on the north elevation.

There are two main ingredients that I use for foliage, rubberised horsehair and Woodland Scenics coarse turf ground foam (not net). The horsehair has a very open and spongey appearance, which will provide a structure or foundation for the leaves. I tear off enough pieces about the size of a 2 cm cube, to cover the tree. These will then need to be pulled apart to make them more open and less uniform in shape. The size varies a little but they open out to between 2 and 4 cm in length.

Adding the leaves starts by filling a jar with a mixture of different coloured coarse ground Woodland Scenics foam. I tend to add a little light and dark green to a base of 50% medium green, as you will find the light green too light for trees on its own. This mixture is shaken around in the jar so that it isn't compressed. I then prepare a table with a covering of newspaper, onto which the pieces of horsehair are laid. To give me a light and delicate ball of green I use Display Mount glue again, as it will penetrate the horsehair and secure the flock to its innermost depths. Picking up a piece of horsehair in a pair of old tweezers. I spray one side and then the other, before dipping and shaking it into the jar of flock. Another quick shake will remove any excess before it is left

Rubberised horsehair as bought in a block from a model shop.

to dry. Producing these foliage sub assemblies has the advantage of controlling the spray adhesive which might otherwise contaminate the trunk and branches. It also enables the foliage to be placed 'inside' the tree and each pad

A delicate pad of foliage results once the horsehair is sprayed with glue and dipped in flock.

can be teased out to produce the desired effect.

A few dabs of Evostik or Bostik contact adhesive on the btanches will secure the foliage pads (*Fig. 61*). Some may need pulling apart a little more, but most

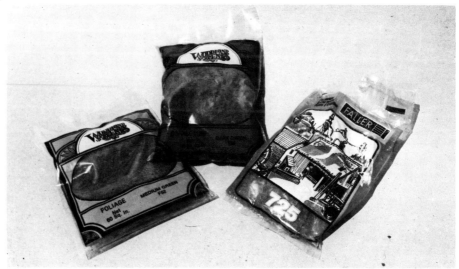

Coarse turf foam flock is best for foliage, not the foliage net or rayon flock.

Just one tree, carefully but simply modelled, will enhance a statement being made about the landscape.

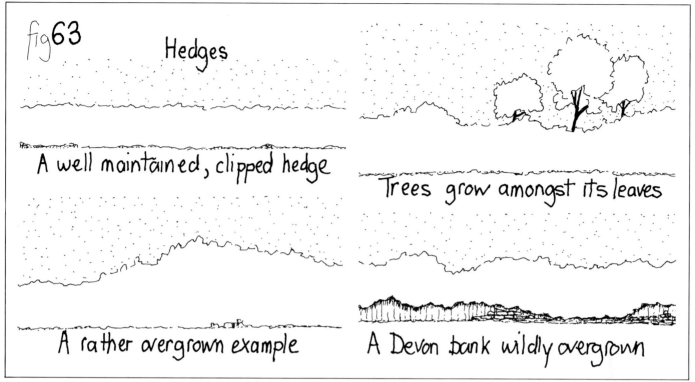

fig63 Hedges

A well maintained, clipped hedge

Trees grow amongst its leaves

A rather overgrown example

A Devon bank wildly overgrown

will capture very simply and effectively the delicate greenness of summer. All that remains to be done is to push the spike on the base of the tree through a hole in the scenery, before securing it in place with a ball of plastic padding.

HEDGES

It is hard to imagine that once 70% of our country was woodland which has been progressively cleared to leave a mere 9% today. This great change in the appearance of our landscape has taken place over the centuries and was brought about by the demands of agriculture and early iron smelting industries. The miles of hedgerows stretching from county to county are also subject to change. New methods of husbandry pressured a move towards enclosing land, and brought about the birth of our hedges and this can be traced back to the mid-fifteenth century. However, enclosure didn't really gather momentum until Georgian times and today larger farms and mechanisation are rapidly reversing the trend.

Hawthorn was the most commonly planted shrub which gathered as its neighbours elder, bramble, blackthorn and dog rose. Of course if the land could not support this growth, walls of stone were carefully engineered over the bleaker and higher fells. I tend to think of hedges as being divided into two basic types, a

common hedge growing at ground level across a field, and the type involving banking, which is common in the West Country. The latter is formed by dividing fields with a bank of earth retained by stones. These Devon banks were planted with shrubs, which having grown over the sides, make it look rather like a large hedge but with a more varied appearance, with areas of stone appearing at some

length, often rich in bracken flowing and cascading over the top and sides.

Management of hedges affect their appearance, neglected ones often growing into trees. A hedge in winter will reveal the care it has received. The old method of 'laying' a hedge to stimulate new growth and make it stock proof, has now largely been superseded by mechanical pollarding. In short, there are many

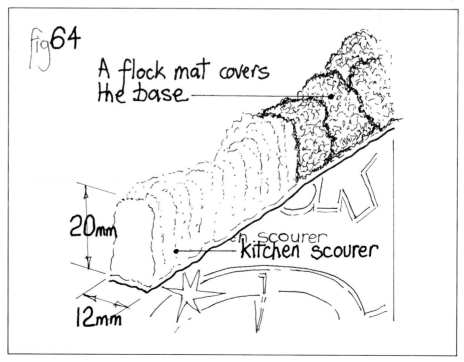

fig64

A flock mat covers the base

20mm

12mm

kitchen scourer

Hedges, whether they cling to hillsides or border lanes, have to be typical of the area being modelled.

A core of pan scourer is covered in a scenic net.

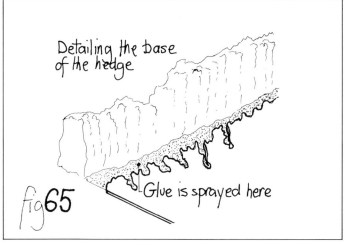

varieties of the simple hedge (*Fig. 63*), and as they are often such a prominent feature of our landscape, it will pay to model them carefully.

Hedges can be made very easily and effectively using an industrial floor polishing pad (which looks much like a giant pan scourer and should be grey or black in colour) as a base. The coarser the pad the better, but if you cannot get hold of one of these from a friendly caretaker, I have also used a pan scourer called 'Brisk' which can be cut up to form the base for about two feet of hedging.

I cut these pads into strips about 20 mm wide, trying to vary the size. It could be cut parallel for a neatly clipped hedge, or very unevenly for a more overgrown type. You will find that it should be about 12 mm thick (*Fig. 64*). Once the strip is ready, I pull it about a little to break it up and vary its density, before gluing it across a field with contact adhesive such as Evostik.

This twiggy base will sprout into life with a covering of greenery, using Woodland Scenics foliage mats. I pull off a piece at a time and stretch it out and glue it over the scouring pad with PVA. The basic colour I use is medium green, but small areas of dark green can be added to represent darker shrubs like brambles.

Details like a spindly tree are easily twisted from a few strands of wire and planted in the top to give the appearance of an overgrown hedge. Moss can also be

Careful detailing along the base of hedgerows completes the impact they have upon the whole landscape.

Beneath banks of weeds the lane winds steeply downhill. Notice the crushed stone surface represented with Marleytex paint.

applied to represent bracken. The detailing can be quite complex, with strands of sisal string and jute adding differing textures. Stones, carved from Polyfilla, can be cut to show the remains of the old bank, along the base of Devon hedges.

If a hedge is just sat on a field, it looks wrong. It needs all the nettles, thistles and long grasses that find shelter and flourish along its roots. I lay a base for this detailing by sprinkling coarse Woodland Scenics flock powder on the ground. First, however, glue has to be applied and I cut a jagged edge to a piece of card, and use this to mask the field when spraying glue between it and the base of the hedge (*Fig. 65*). On top of this jute and sisal are brought into use again to represent docks, thistles and nettles. A little carpet underfelt forms long grass and the whole scene appears more complete.

LANES

The railway certainly intruded upon the web of lanes that twisted and turned between village and farm. By necessity the railway was carried over and burrowed under these rights of way, a concept that must be acknowledged and alluded to in our model making. Some of the earliest

lanes were barely the width of a cart, whilst others were much wider. Some are hidden beneath banks of fern, whereas others stand proud beside dykes and fields. Thus the nature of the lanes and roads in any location also needs careful investigation, to capture the authentic character of a region.

The Cornish lanes around Petherick are a modest 45 mm in width and surfaced with the textured paint (Marleytex) applied to the whole landscape as already described. Remember that today's surface of tarmac is a recent luxury to the rural countryside where even today many lanes are unmetalled. A surface treatment that captures the appearance of crushed stone is therefore more appropriate to my Edwardian setting.

The surface of the lane will need colouring and the crushed stone I am representing has to be kept a fairly light grey shade. However, it is worth bearing in mind that most road and yard surfaces are bleached by the sun and on dry days even 'black' tarmac can be an extremely pale grey. I use Artists Water Colours, mainly Davy's Grey, adding a few areas of Burnt Sienna and Sap Green to represent mud and a trace of moss and weeds. It is important that all the colours blend

together to give a subtle overall impression. Study the surface you wish to represent and try and view it in your chosen weather conditions. Remember simple things, for instance, near farm gates far more mud will have been trampled out of the field and rolled into the road, and under hanging trees the surface may well be a darker colour from the fallen rain and moisture that takes longer to dry in the sunshine.

The effect of a rain storm in changing colours is quite dramatic. Colours darken rapidly and that tarmac road may revert to a dark grey, and mud (once a light greyish brown) becomes a rich dark brown. Remember also that colours will appear darker to you the nearer they are. It is no use mixing up a paint and comparing it to the road outside your home, the effect of scale and distance will make it much, much paler, as it fades into the background.

Many effects make for a more interesting model, like the marks of cart wheels, particularly at the entrances to fields. Some hardly used lanes or cart tracks may be well endowed with grass and broken stones. Here the rumbling of cart wheels will clear a track and leave a path through the encroaching green. The most

A quiet lane leads travellers towards the station. It has a purpose and appears to have been established before the railway.

A colourful hedgerow and welcome signpost complete the laneside scene.

important thing to remember is that everything should blend together, even the colours of the lane and the hue of the grass and hedges in the surrounding land.

Look to the side of the road for banks covered with bracken or long grass, tease out pieces of carpet felt and glue down moss. It would be exciting to capture the delicate lacy white cow parsley as it clouds the verges of lanes in May, or perhaps a mass of wild flowers throwing colour from neighbouring hedgerow (*Fig. 66*).

FENCES

Railway companies erected miles of fencing to keep humans and livestock off the track and protect their property. This all too obvious part of the railway scene is frequently modelled very badly. Wooden five-bar fences or posts strung with wires were the most common types, but in many bleak counties drystone walls served the same purpose. It is therefore necessary to establish the type used around your railway and look for a way of representing it.

I have always used the plastic wooden fencing manufactured by Ratio, but have been careful to use it with some thought. The days of using strips of balsa are thankfully over, but it did attract a lot of favourable comment by those who

thought that a railway fence should be nicely broken and dilapidated, which of course it should not be.

To use the Ratio product I first file down the surface of the five bars to remove the roundness caused in their manufacture. This makes quite a difference and is such a simple improvement to make. When it comes to gluing the fence

around the layout, remember above all else, that the posts were always sunk into the soil vertically (*Fig. 67*). So many people seem to forget this, and the difference is very noticeable. It is therefore necessary to bend the fence to follow a hillside, and the best way I have found is to hold each side of the post between my finger and thumb, pulling until the

fig 66

A web of cow parsley stands beside a lane

correct angle is found (*Fig. 68*). It does take a little time to move along the length of a fence, but the result is worthwhile. Glue the fence down with the rails facing the inside or railway side of the fence. Paint them a light greyish brown colour, the shade of timber as it weathers. I would avoid any dark brown fences as even recent creosoted timbers would certainly appear lighter from a distance. Add some green moss, a few streaks of brown with a selection of greys, to make a more varied appearance, and perhaps even a greedy blackbird looking for a worm, or a seagull perching on a post. Complete the scene by gluing flock with a few strands of sisal string along the base of the fence, making it appear tangled in grass and weeds (*Fig. 68a*).

GATES AND GATEWAYS

It is worth considering what happens around the entrance to a field. It is the place that humans look in and the sheep and cattle look out, and this idle traffic wears the grass around the gateway and

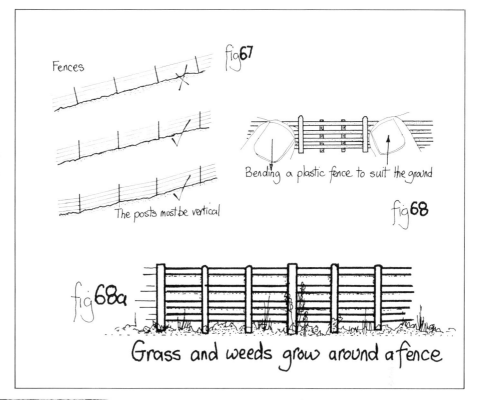

This lineside fencing has been carefully bent to match the contour of the land.

It is surprising how improved the appearance of a fence becomes, if it is bedded in a tangle of long grass and weeds.

produces the rutted nature of the ground, wet and boggy underfoot in winter.

With this in mind I scrape away the lint around this area and try to make it well worn. A screwdriver can be forced in to make ruts in the Mod Roc surface and a little Polyfilla can enhance the effect. To blend the earth colour into the grass, I paint on washes of a grey/brown water colour, a mixture of Davy's Grey and Burnt Sienna. Water tends to settle in these deep ruts which are therefore coloured a darker brown, gradually fading to the drier surrounding grey/brown hue. Again it is here that we see so clearly the changes in colour that water makes. It can be effective to finish the scene by squeezing some polystyrene cement into the ruts to form puddles.

Gates can be bought as mouldings or castings but really convincing ones of

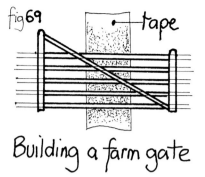

fig 69 — tape

Building a farm gate

scale appearance can be made up from strips of Plastikard. Again a field trip is the best source of inspiration, just measure up the gate you choose. Strips of 0.020 inch Plastikard can be used for the bars and this can be tacked to a board with double-sided tape (*Fig. 69*) while the cross members and posts are glued in place. Only cut the gate free when every-

thing is dry. Remember that gates will generally be shut, and although some were white, they are best painted in much the same way as the railway companies' wooden fencing.

THE STATION GARDEN

If you have ever been to Pendon Museum and seen the cottage gardens modelled there, you cannot help but be left with a lasting memory of exquisite modelling. I cannot pretend that my station garden is a patch on theirs, but I hope the simple and quick methods I use capture something of an English country garden.

I found that when building a layout the size of Petherick, I could not always spend as many hours as I would have liked on some aspects of the detailing. Therefore, what I am about to describe is more of an impression, a scene in late

The passing of cart wheels and hooves has worn away the grass and rutted the muddy ground through the gateway.

An impression of the depth and length of the complete model.

July or early August. The first thing to establish is the month of the year, otherwise you may have the station master picking a bunch of tulips and sweet peas for his wife, whilst digging up his leeks for dinner!

The easiest thing to model is a lawn. To get that smooth neatly cut appearance I use rayon flock (Noch Flock) glued down to a bed of PVA glue. Remember that the colour will vary from a rich green if it has been wet, to a parched yellow and brown in a hot summer. Use oil-based paint like the Humbrol range to create this impression. You could detail this with a lawn mower for the station master to push, in the days before the peace of our Sunday mornings was broken by the whirl of strimmers and Flymos.

Adding a border of flowers can be approached with a variety of techniques. The quickest is to glue down small lumps of lichen, and to dab on fluorescent paint (*Fig. 70a*). You will find that normal yellow, red and blue paint will look very

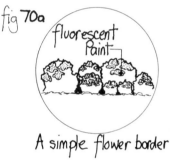

A simple flower border

dull from a distance, but fluorescent colours inject a vivid sparkle to the flora. Additional texture can be added by careful application of tissue paper for petals and flock powder for leaves, adding more depth and interest to the scene. Likewise, a herbaceous border with irises, hollyhocks and gladioli introduces new shapes and height, establishing more variety, colour and texture (*Fig. 70b*). These are easy to model using the bristles from a broom. They are dipped into PVA glue and then foam flock, and after a trim and a few dabs of colour they are ready for planting. Similarly sisal string, another useful material, can masquerade as tulips, daffodils, Esther Reads, poppies and sweet William. By planting one hair, and adding a dab of flock on the top, an array of flower heads will bloom when painted.

I'm sure every garden had its vegetable patch, particularly in years gone by, and jolly interesting things they are to make.

A simple but effective station garden.   BOB COCKROFT

Chris Pilton, an eminent member of the Pendon team, wrote a fascinating account of how he produced the ultimate 4mm scale vegetable plot in *Model Railway Journal* No. 5. However, these are rather fiddly things to model and very time consuming so I will describe my admittedly cruder, but simpler method. I cut a piece of card the size of the plot, cover it with a greyish brown flock and build everything up onto this. At Petherick the station master's runner beans were added first, as their size and shape soon adds character and interest to the muddy plot. Again the hard bristle brush was used for canes, which were cut about 30 mm long. They were then dipped in glue and given a sparse covering of green foam, before being left to dry. With a pair of tweezers and much patience, the framework of canes was assembled and finished with a few dabs of orange paint to represent the flowers (*Fig. 71*).

The station master was also picking the last of his spring cabbages which he

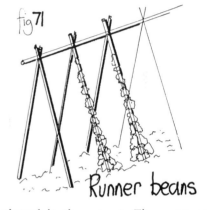

Runner beans

planted in the autumn. They were now quite large and modelled from coloured paper handkerchiefs. I cut two discs for the large outer leaves and screwed up balls for the hearts (*Fig. 71a*). They were assembled by gluing the leaves around the hearts, staggering them slightly. A wash of bluish/green water colour tinted them, and I'm sure a row of these will guarantee

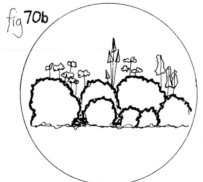

Added shapes, colours and textures

A cabbage

the station master first prize in the village show.

He may also be as lucky with his Stuttguard Giants (onions for those who spend their summers model-making rather than gardening). The bulb should only be about 1mm in diameter once fully grown, and would be half buried in the soil. I used grains of rice, cutting them in half for this, and sisal string for the leaves. Remember that in late August these tops will be bent over, and a different colour to the earlier green.

These are just a few suggestions, as vegetable gardening is just a matter of experimenting with different materials, until the best effects and impressions are achieved. Don't forget the potting shed, wheel-barrow, compost heap and spade standing in the ground. You could even have a few pigeons eating the tops out of the cabbages, and sparrows pecking at bread thrown out on to the lawn by the station master's wife.

THE STATION PLATFORM

The time to build the platforms and goods docks is once the track is laid and before the scenery is started. Although their construction is quite straight-forward, a number of questions always

seem to arise that need answering before a start can be made.

You may wonder how wide a platform is. Passenger-carrying lines had to conform to certain standards laid down by the Board of Trade and before being opened to the public they underwent a rigorous inspection. When Colonel Yolland inspected the E & WJ Railway for the Board of Trade, he complained that the up platform at Fenny Compton was not the requisite minimum of 6 feet at one point, in fact it was only 2 feet 11 inches. Height is just as important so it is perhaps wise to investigate the proto-type more fully in the location being

modelled; the accompanying diagram will give some guide to these minimum dimensions (*Fig. 72a*).

On the prototype, the sides of the platform are built first and likewise by cutting strips of softwood or chipboard to the height required, we can build the sides of the model. These are glued along the edge of the track far enough away to allow for necessary clearances and the thickness of any cladding that may be glued to its face (*Fig. 72b*). The design of the platform will vary greatly from railway to railway; it may be faced in coursed or random stone, concrete or brick, and edged in bricks or large slabs

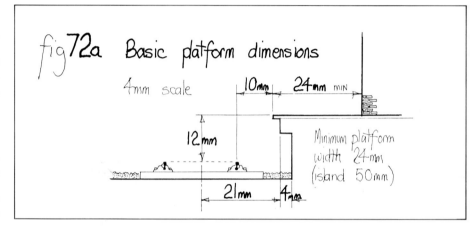

The stone-faced platforms of North Cornwall clad with Wills Finecast plastic coarse stone sheets.

Silver birches reflect in the shallow still waters of a pond by a lonely lane.

S. H. FREESE

of stone, or built entirely from timbers. There can be no better answer than to look at a few photographs to gain an understanding of how they are built in the locality selected for the model.

Once a framework of strips has been built up, the top surface is cut from 1.5 mm birch ply and glued in place. On to this, a simple textured surface representing gravel and ash will need to be added, and I found Slater's scenic dressings (flock powder) ideal for this purpose. It has the appearance of very fine sawdust and the natural wood colour (SC/4 Dead Grass) provides a good base to paint. It is sprinkled over a layer of undiluted PVA glue, and when dry given a very thin wash of grey paint (Humbrol enamel or Precision) until the shade of the prototype is matched. Washes of brown and a little dry brushed green, grey and mud will bring the surface to life before the edging stones and details can be added to complete the model.

STREAMS, PONDS & RIVER BANKS

The Willow Brook, which trickles at the bottom of our garden through an avenue of hawthorn and elder, is home for a family of moorhens and an elusive pair of kingfishers, and also provides a welcoming habitat for water voles and the occasional mallard. This quiet haven contrasts sharply with the rushing of moorland streams and flowing waters of the Nene, its mother river. Such streams, brooks and rivers are fascinating subjects to model, each with its own character and uniqueness that makes generalization in a modelling book difficult. However, there are two things that we are going to

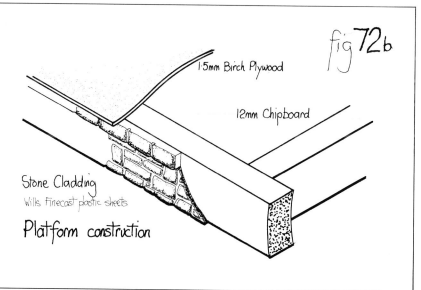

fig 72b

1·5mm Birch Plywood

12mm Chipboard

Stone Cladding
Wills Finecast plastic sheets

Platform construction

The calm water of this mill pond slips through sluices past rushes and reeds on this magnificent scene from Pendon Museum. The water is represented by a sheet of perspex painted black underneath.
A. E. SMITH

look at, banks and the flow of water over the stream or river bed.

The shape and appearance of banks are determined by the flow of the water and which side of a bend they are on. A fast flowing river will clean the outside bank and undercut it as it rushes around a bend, whereas the inside bank can be very gentle, silted and shallow. Steep-sided banks will have already been modelled into the basic landscape shell, but can now be detailed with a textured layer of Polyfilla. At the top, grass overhangs with weeds and bullrushes in the water below, calling for careful use of sisal string, jute and the hard bristle brush (*Fig. 73a*). As a contrast, a shallow water's edge soon becomes a watering place for livestock. Here the grass will be worn away and the

hoofprints of many cattle, impressed into the mud (*Fig. 73b*). Somewhere in the middle of these two types must be the overgrown bank, rich in small trees, bushes and shrubs where the damp soil encourages a healthy growth of plants and weeds, safe from the ploughing of fields and roaming animals. Trees can be particularly spectacular in spring when the delicate May blossom, pink and white, shelters the waters below. A layer of carpet felt will give a sound base onto which small trees, twisted from wire, can be planted.

A steep bank

fig 73a

Bullrushes and reeds

fig 73b

A shallow riverbank

The bed of a river or stream can be textured with sand and small stones before adding rushes and weeds. Perhaps an old bike or pram, rusting and entangled in the reeds, will enhance a scene. Different techniques can be adopted to represent water. For the shallowest of streams, polyurethene gloss varnish painted coat by coat over the detail, will capture well, the trickling water. However, for a deeper effect, casting resin mixed and poured between the banks would be better. Remember to seal up the ends of the stream or river before pouring in the resin, and perhaps use two layers. An interesting effect results if streaks of matt white oil paint (Humbrol) are added as it dries. If the finished water is too clean, a wash with a greyish green paint will pollute it, and the sparkle of the surface can be reintroduced with a coat of gloss varnish.

There are many very well modelled examples of water. The quiet and still village pond at Pendon contrasts with the water lapping over the sandy banks on the East Suffolk Light. These are examples that highlight this interesting subject better than my limited experience, and are well worth studying.

LIVESTOCK

Model cats, dogs, sheep, cows and pigs thankfully can be bought as metal castings or plastic mouldings. In most cases a touch of paint will finish them, but it is worth considering what can be done to improve them. Bulls could have their horns sharpened with wire, and the more stocky breeds of cattle fattened with a covering of plastic padding. This may seem unnecessary, but certain breeds of cattle were associated with one county, and it may therefore help to establish the true location of your model. A Devon Red is more appropriate in the West Country, and an Aberdeen Angus in the Highlands. Today's Friesian that roam our present hillsides date only from the 'thirties, so for pre-grouping modelling the now rarer breeds should be seen.

When painting animals it is important to finish them with a very matt, and slightly rough surface. It is easy to achieve this if talcum powder is mixed with the paint until it becomes thick and sticky. This is dabbed on the animal, then highlighted by mixing tints and shades of the base colour. Eyes and other small details can be painted with the point of a

Now rare breeds, but then commonplace and often unique to one county. S. H. FREESE

pin, until the completed model resembles a photograph of its breed. It is perhaps worth mentioning that I usually hold the animals by gluing them to a strip of wood. This is easier than holding their legs in tweezers or your fingers.

When it comes to placing them in a field, consider how they graze. Sheep tend to be dotted about a hillside, and only gather together when being rounded up by a collie. Cattle, on the other hand, will stick together, perhaps in small groups, and their positions generally relate to one another.

VILLAGE LIFE

A chat at the postbox, meeting Aunt Hilda from the 10.15, or Rags, the border collie, rounding up a flock of sheep, are just a few little scenes that add village life

to your model. After all, it it wasn't for the local community, there wouldn't be a need for the railway at all.

People, by the way they dress reflect a time in our history. Fortunately it is now possible to buy cast figures in different poses and fashion, sculptured in periods from the turn of the century to the present day. Again a little research will be needed to find out about colours and patterns on clothes, so they fit in to the authenticity of a period piece. Again when painting them, don't use gloss or semi-gloss paints; if needs be, mix talcum powder with the paint to give it a textured but flat finish. Don't paint faces pink — look, and you will see that particularly from a distance they appear very white. A yellowish tint, perhaps with a touch of pink is the most appropriate colour. Like

A modelled scene should be as natural and uncontrived as this. S. H. FREESE

animals, it is easier to paint these fiddly items if they are first glued to a stick, then they can be handled more easily (*Fig. 75*). Military modellers are generally way ahead in this field and often produce exceptionally convincing results. I mention this because we could all learn a lot from them and many good railway models are spoilt by poor figures.

Try to glue them onto the layout in meaningful poses, talking, arguing,

Life as it was, uncluttered, unspectacular, but authentic and full of atmosphere.　　S. H. FREESE

We should capture scenes as they were, and not how we think they were. A working traction engine in the quiet seclusion of a field. S. H. FREESE

Telegraph poles — a vital part of any railway scene.   J. H. VENN

explaining, and position these groups in relation to other objects such as the corner of a building, by a postbox, or under a tree. In this way scenes will look more real, and details will appear purposeful and not fragmented.

Lastly, the choice of road vehicles and farm implements will immediately give an onlooker many clues as to the period of the model. A landau meeting the express from Exeter would in later years be replaced by a taxi. Similarly, a reaper or binder would be superseded by a combine harvester, and a traction engine by a tractor. The presence of traction engines and steam rollers on many models (often immaculate and over-glossy) has become rather a cliché. Even in their heyday these work horses were not to be seen on every street corner, station forecourt and goods yard. It might therefore be more authentic if you wish to feature one of these costly machines to show one discreetly tucked away under a tarpaulin at the edge of a field, farmyard, or roadworks. Understatement is often far more convincing.

There is a wide and varied range of white metal kits of varying quality and authenticity for motor cars and farming machinery, so there should be little

excuse, in 4mm scale, for an out of period vehicle. Some are more delicate and convincing than others, but care must be taken when colouring even the best of them. A trip to a rural life museum or a browse through the pages of a book will help you to be more authentic.

TELEGRAPH POLES

Have you ever wondered how far apart telegraph poles should be placed along your layout? Information like this is vital if such a visually important railway feature is to be modelled convincingly. The railway companies compromised between the need to reduce the number of poles (because of their cost and the fact that each insulator was a source of leakage), and possible excessive sag in the wires with the risk of accidental contact if the span was too great. Examples can give a guide. On the GWR the spacing was originally 73 yard spans (24 posts to the mile), later reduced to 55 yards (32 posts to the mile) when heavier gauge wire was adopted. On the LNER 65 yards was regarded as the average, reduced to 60 or even 50 yards on curves, and a span of more than 70 yards was regarded as exceptional. The pole route generally followed the inside of a curve so that a

dislodged wire or pole would fall away from the running lines. Spacing was as even as possible, but at the crossing of a road or railway lines, the span was kept as short as possible.

As it was desirable to keep the wires at a fairly constant height above rail level, the height of the poles would vary — shorter in cuttings and taller on embankments. The height would have to rise over roads, railways and tunnels, although in the latter case cabling was often used to route the wires through the bore (the wires terminating and running down a pole then along the ground in conduit). The minimum heights for the lowest wires were 16 ft above occupation crossings, 17 ft above railways and 20 ft above the level of a main road. Poles varied in height, between 20 ft and 50 ft or more, and the higher poles with many wires were often doubled up into an 'A' pole or 'H' pole for greater strength. Terminal poles, for example where a pole route ended at a tunnel mouth, were often square and sometimes carried a wooden finial. Some companies, notably the Midland and the GWR, used square posts as the norm on certain pole routes.

Within a station area, there must be at least one 'lead-off' pole, usually adjacent to the signal box, where insulated wires were terminated with the open wires and led down the pole to the instruments. Wires were needed not only for the telegraph (and later telephone) circuits, but also for the block telegraph and signal repeaters. A 'lead-off' pole was similarly required at each lineside location which had an electrical connection — track circuit end or signal which could not be seen by the signalman and required a repeater in the signal box. 'Lead-off' poles beside station buildings were often painted — typically black for the first four feet from the ground, then a pale colour above. Otherwise poles were left in creosoted finish, which weathered to a pale grey or light brown appearance when dry; the poles only appeared dark brown on a rainy day.

Undoubtedly the best source of information is photographs which are always worth studying. However, I hope these notes will be a guide towards what to look for. Of course scratch-built poles built to individual needs will be most rewarding, but even adaptations to commercially manufactured poles like those by Dapol (ex Airfix) are worthwhile.

A backscene should not take the eye away from the model but should help to complete the elusion of depth.

CHAPTER FIVE

Presentation of a Landscaped Model

PAINTING BACKSCENES

I wouldn't contemplate building a model landscape now without a backscene. A model looks so much better if surrounded by a backcloth of hills which contributes immensely to the illusion of depth. Once this was often considered an optional extra, avoided by all except the talented artist. However, a simple country backscene need not be a difficult task, provided a few simple rules are followed.

The key to landscape painting is the horizon, the important line twixt sky and ground. The laws of perspective state that this line is at your eye level and around it the rest of the landscape is formed. As an example, if you take a view of the sea and stand, lie down, or climb to the top of a cliff, the horizon is still at the level of your eye. What changes is your view of everything else. Imagine looking at a person standing on the beach. If you are also standing, you meet eye to eye; if you

are lying down, you look up at him, and if you are standing on a cliff, you are looking down on his head, but in each case the horizon is at your eye level.

A countryside scene can be analysed in much the same way. Hills will rise above the horizon, and distant objects diminish in size towards it. However, theory is to some extent unimportant in our case as what I am going to recommend is a step by step approach to drawing a scene that will give an impression of distant hills, fields, hedges and trees.

A practice piece will not be wasted, so on a piece of cartridge paper draw a fairly straight line to represent the horizon. Then pin this to the back of your layout and go to the front and look across at it. Decide whether it looks too high or too low and alter its position until it looks right. Draw the line where the backscene and layout meet (*Fig. 77a*). Split the gap between these two lines in half and then split the top gap in half again. In this way

the lines of hedges bordering the fields appear to be getting closer together (*Fig. 77b*). Finally, divide these parallel strips into triangles and diamonds, not too many, to represent a patchwork of fields (*Fig. 77c*). The width of the hedges can be increased so that the near hedges are much larger than the distant ones. The outlines of trees can be pencilled in, giving us a very simplified, but realistic landscape picture (*Fig. 77d*).

When you have achieved a satisfying result, pin a long strip of paper around your layout, and repeat the process. Avoid complicating the drawing with buildings, especially if they are seen obliquely. This would involve the techniques of two point perspective to capture the diminishing effect on their walls (*Fig. 78a*). However, it may not be so easy to overlook lanes or roads that disappear into the background. Simply remember that they should never be parallel, they disappear towards a single

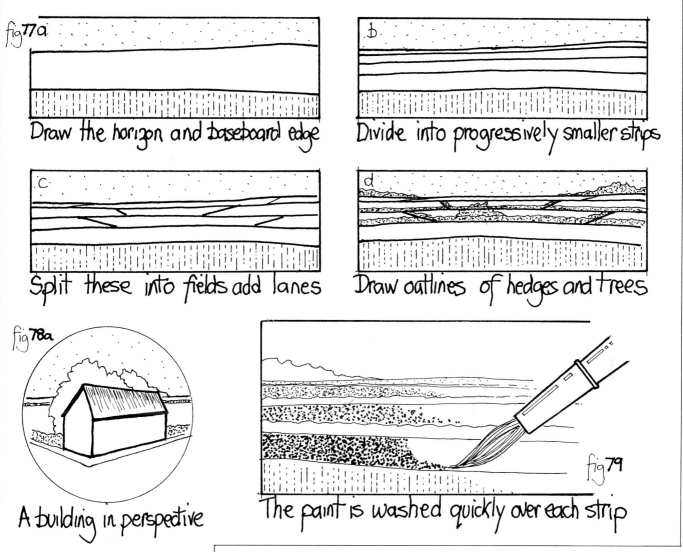

fig 77 a

Draw the horizon and baseboard edge

b

Divide into progressively smaller strips

C

Split these into fields add lanes

d

Draw outlines of hedges and trees

fig 78a

A building in perspective

fig 79

The paint is washed quickly over each strip

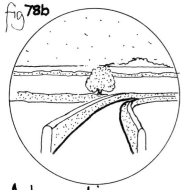

fig 78b

A lane disappears

vanishing point on the horizon. However, in reality, they never reach the horizon, they twist and turn, changing their direction (*Fig. 78b*).

Painting the scene need not be difficult. We are going to use a technique called colour washing, which, as the name suggests, involves washing over the paper with a very watery layer of paint. I mix up 4 dabs of Sap Green and 1 dab each of Dark Hooker Green and Burnt Sienna. Add plenty of water to make the mix flow over the paper, and wash it over the bottom layer of fields. Add more water and wash the next layer, before adding even more water to paint the next (*Fig. 79*). What should appear is a gradual lightening cover of green, fading towards the horizon. Experiment, use plenty of water and remember that a wash if too light, can be painted over again, once it is dry. however, a wash that is too dark cannot be lightened, so aim to make the

mix too weak. Yellows and browns need not be introduced to represent crops or ploughed fields, as distant colours are both weak and grey.

Trees and hedges were painted with the same mix, but with far less water, dabbing, rather than washing the colour on the picture. Distant trees tend to appear more blue/grey. These techniques will not make you a Constable or Monet, but they will provide an easy way of achieving an effective backscene.

This background of fields is cut out and left to one side while the sky is prepared. I didn't attempt to paint a sky, as I thought it more sensible to make use of the printed paper that is sold in rolls at many model shops. I cut the backing for the backscene from hardboard and glued the sky paper to it. To prevent any wrinkles, I used photomount glue, spraying it onto the wood, and gradually unrolling the sky and smoothing it into

By using a curved backscene, this unsightly view of a corner would have been avoided.

position. The scene was finished by gluing the painted fields over the sky, and the difference this impression of distance has made is immense.

The final appearance of the back cloth can be refined by introducing curves into the corners, as joins between two faces can scar the scene (*Fig. 80*). Similarly it is a good idea to place details on the layout near to the back to help conceal the edge between the baseboard and backscene. However, it is important not to place them so close that they cast shadows over the backscene. This looks most unrealistic (*Fig. 81*).

LIGHTING AND DISPLAY

Having spent so much time and trouble in attempting to create the most realistic scene we can, there are just a few more points that will enrich and improve our model and aid the illusion.

Lighting has a considerable impact in highlighting textures, and bringing a richness out of the colouring. A natural softness to the scene cannot be achieved by the harsh and uncontrolled play of daylight, it needs to be built into the presentation of the layout. The quality of

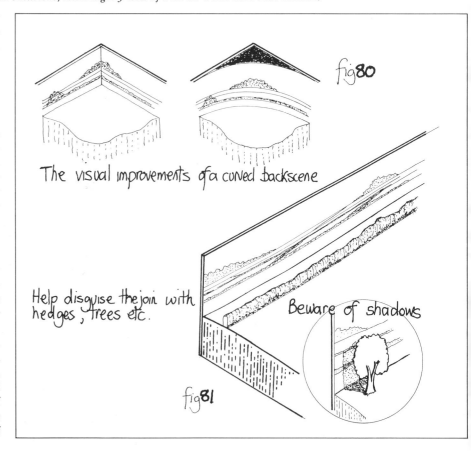

fig 80

The visual improvements of a curved backscene

Help disguise the join with hedges, trees etc.

Beware of shadows

fig 81

By carefully positioning hedges and trees, shadows can be avoided on the backscene, and the join with the backscene disguised.

This untidy view will be less confusing to the eye when a black curtain and fascia panel is added to complete the presentation.

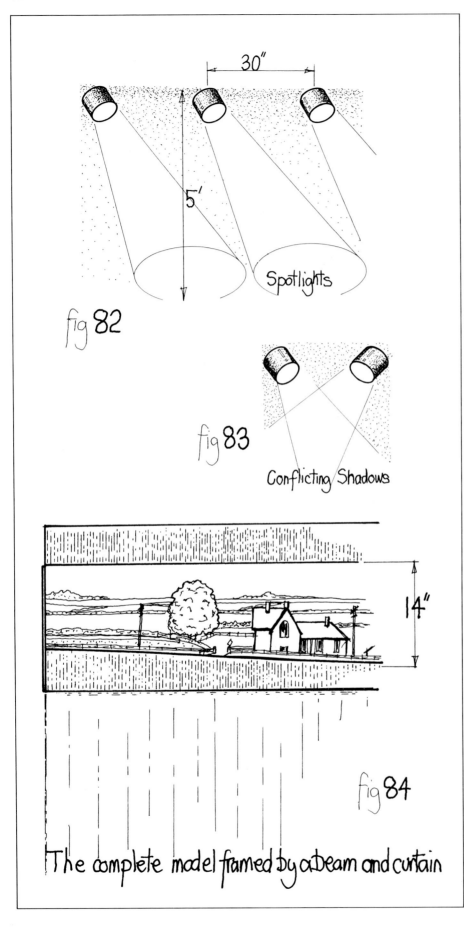

fig 82

fig 83

Conflicting Shadows

fig 84

The complete model framed by a beam and curtain

light very much affects the appearance of the model. Daylight, fluorescent and tungsten filament lighting all make different demands on the balance and tones of colours and textures. Daylight is effective, particularly sunlight, but on a dull day colours change and details are lost. Fluorescent lights also tend to bleach colours and flatten textures. They lack the subtle highlights and shadows that appear when sunlight falls through clouds onto a scene.

Carefully selected spotlights are my choice. When their soft light is controlled and directed it can create shadows and depth. After much experimentation I have found the best results are achieved by using a 60w mini spot bulb, placed about 5 ft (*Fig. 82*) above the model. If it is positioned too low or a more powerful bulb used, the light becomes too intense, and falls upon too small an area. At 5 ft they seem to illuminate about 30 inches of model, so by placing them at this distance they produce a good balanced picture. Remember that sunlight beams through the clouds from the east, through the south and then the west, laying shadows in one direction at a time (*Fig. 83*).

The only disadvantage with spots is the height needed to make them effective. If this is a problem, a normal 40w or 60w line of tungsten filament bulbs could be used instead, but in an enclosed space they will generate much heat.

For a layout built and kept in the home, a good lighting system is worth considering. For an exhibition layout, it is essential. In a dark hall where interference from other light sources is limited, the full richness of your own lighting system can be appreciated.

Curtaining hung below the baseboard will help to improve presentation but to compliment the flow of light, a clear frame around the model will enhance the impact of presentation. A beam placed along the top of the layout will cut out unwanted views of the operators and force a realistic viewing angle (*Fig. 84*). Aerial views will no longer be possible, and the impression of depth will be realised more vividly, as you are directed towards peering into the model. A landscape rolls before you, and the atmosphere of another world is captured in miniature for you to enjoy.

A Modeller's Sketch Pad

I have taken scale track plans of various stations, and presented them in a way that I feel reflects their landscape setting. Very little compression of the layout has taken place, and each station has been chosen to look at a different type of scenic environment. Look at them, think about them. Perhaps they will inspire you to sketch and adapt your own favourite prototypes and start landscape modelling.

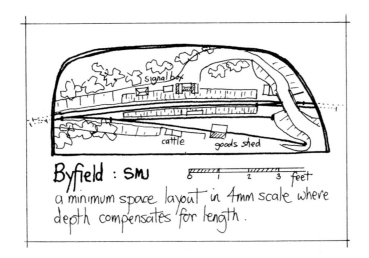

Byfield : SMJ

a minimum space layout in 4mm scale where depth compensates for length.

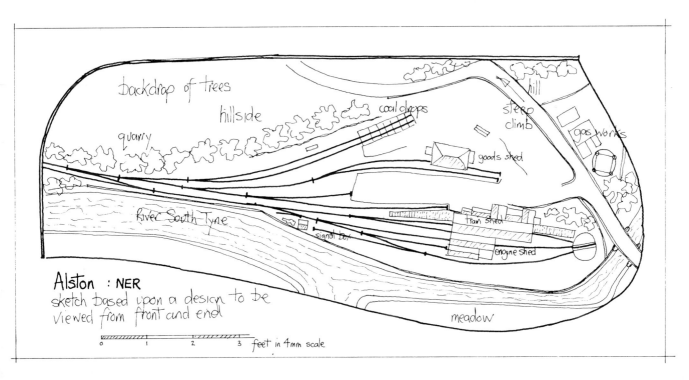

Alston : NER

sketch based upon a design to be viewed from front and end

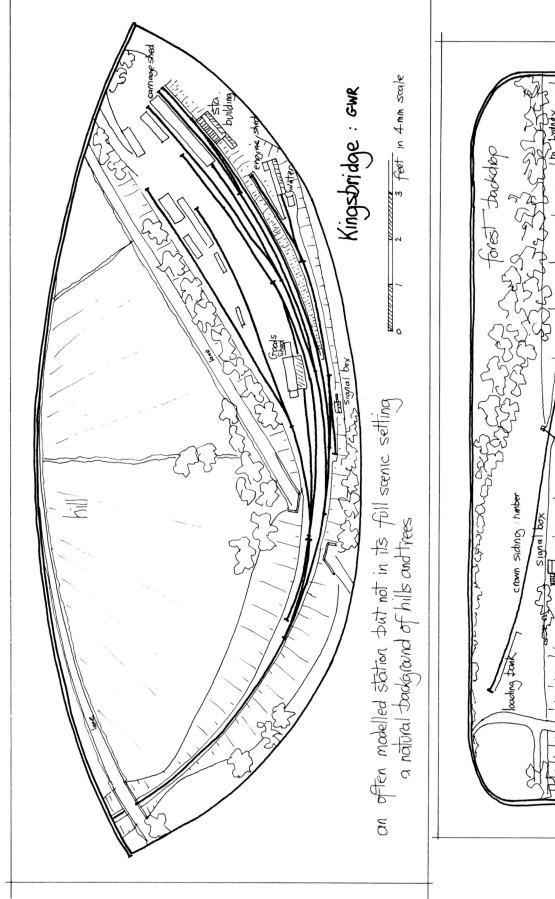

Kingsbridge : GWR

an often modelled station but not in its full scenic setting
a natural background of hills and trees

carriage shed

Sta. building

engine shed

water

Goods Shed

line

signal box

hill

lane

0 1 2 3 feet in 4mm scale

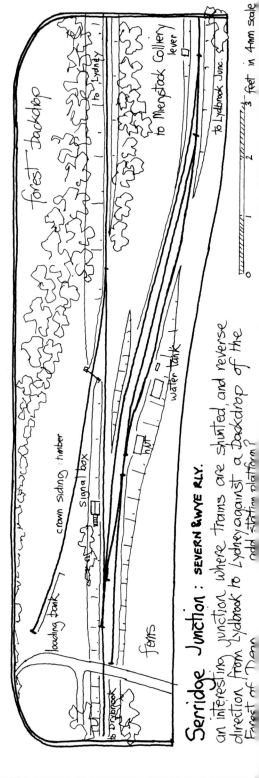

forest backdrop

to Lydney

to Menstock Colliery
lever

to Lydbrook Junc.

crown siding : timber

signal box

water tank

loading bank

ferns

hut

to Drybrook

3 feet in 4mm scale

Serridge Junction : SEVERN &WYE RLY.

an interesting junction where trains are shunted, and reverse
direction from Lydbrook to Lydney against a backdrop of the
Forest of Dean
add station platform?

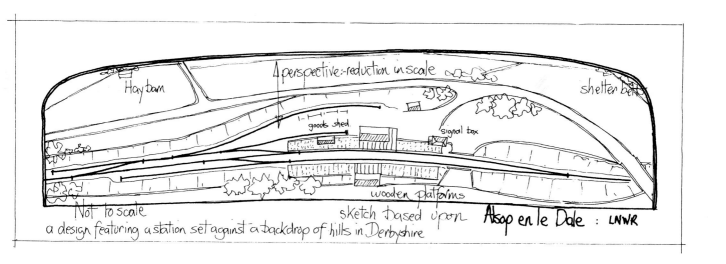

↓ perspective:-reduction in scale

Hay barn

shelter belt

goods shed.

signal box

wooden platforms

Not to scale

sketch based upon   Alsop en le Dale : LNWR

a design featuring a station set against a backdrop of hills in Derbyshire

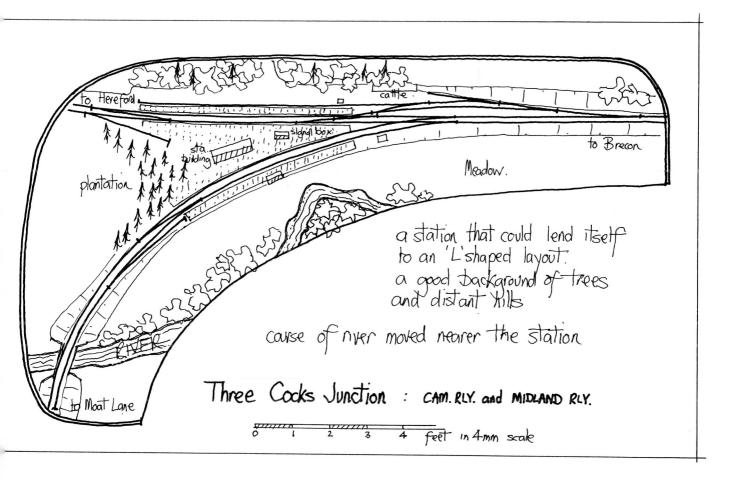

to Hereford

cattle

signal box

sta building

to Brecon

plantation

Meadow.

RIVER

a station that could lend itself
to an 'L' shaped layout.
a good background of trees
and distant hills

cause of river moved nearer the station

to Moat Lane

Three Cocks Junction : CAM. RLY. and MIDLAND RLY.

0   1   2   3   4   feet in 4 mm scale

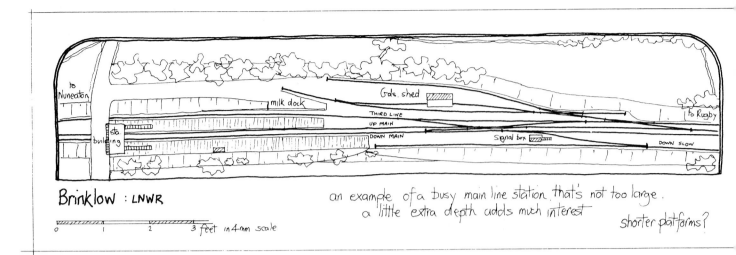

Brinklow : LNWR

0   1   2   3 feet in 4mm scale

an example of a busy main line station that's not too large.
a 'little' extra depth adds much interest

shorter platforms?

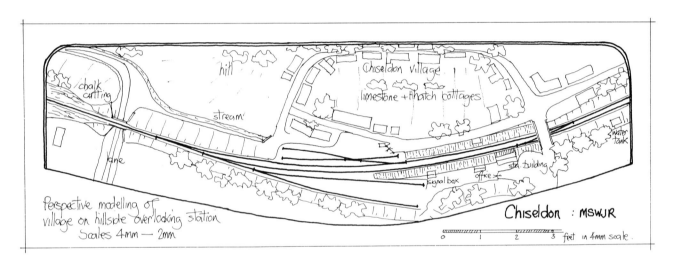

Perspective modelling of
village on hillside overlooking station
Scales 4mm — 2mm

Chiseldon : MSWJR

0   1   2   3 feet in 4mm scale.

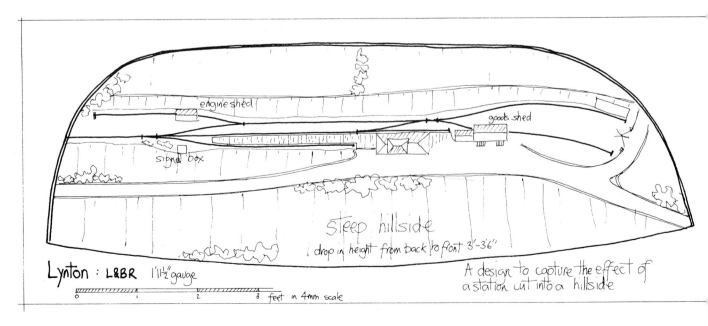

steep hillside
drop in height from back to front 3'–3'6"

Lynton : L&BR   1'1½" gauge

0   1   2   3 feet in 4mm scale

A design to capture the effect of
a station cut into a hillside